Attracting Birds & Butterflies

BARBARA ELLIS

HOW TO PLAN AND PLANT A BACKYARD HABITAT

Copyright © 1997 by Houghton Mifflin Company
Drawings copyright © 1997 by Steve Buchanan

For information about permission to reproduce selections from this book,
write to Permissions, Houghton Mifflin Company, 215 Park Avenue South,
New York, New York 10003.

For information about this and other Houghton Mifflin trade
and reference books and multimedia products, visit The Bookstore at
Houghton Mifflin on the World Wide Web at http://www.hmco.com/trade/.

Taylor's Guide is a registered trademark of Houghton Mifflin Company.

Library of Congress Cataloging-in-Publication Data

Ellis, Barbara W.
Attracting birds and butterflies / Barbara Ellis.
     p. cm. — (Taylor's weekend gardening guides)
   Includes index.
   ISBN 0-395-81372-7
   1. Gardening to attract birds. 2. Butterfly gardening.
   I. Title. II. Series.
  QL676.5.E57 1997
  635.9'6—dc20   97-25443

Printed in the United States of America.

RMT 10 9 8 7 6 5 4 3 2 1

Book design by Deborah Fillion
Cover photograph © by Dwight R. Kuhn

CONTENTS

To songbirds, hummingbirds, butterflies, and other wildlife, the typical suburban landscape resembles an unfriendly desert. Close-cropped lawns, sheared foundation shrubs, and deadheaded flowers mean no place to nest, no food to eat, and nowhere to hide. Fortunately, any landscape can become a haven for winged wildlife — and for the people that share it. Wildlife-friendly yards and gardens are filled with flowers from spring to frost, brilliant berries, and glistening water — along with dazzling birds and butterflies. Since lower maintenance is another advantage, it's easy to see how both wildlife and people benefit. Use this book as a guide to help you plant a landscape that welcomes winged wildlife. In the process, you'll create a garden that enriches your own life as well.

In winter, a female cardinal is attracted to a heavily laden branch of pyracantha berries.

Chapter 1:
Welcoming Winged Wildlife

Creating a garden that welcomes songbirds, hummingbirds, and butterflies may seem like a confusing and complicated task, but the principles involved are relatively simple. In essence, birds and butterflies need the same basic things you do to feel at home in a new place — they just define them a little differently. First and foremost, they need a ready supply of food. While you expect a well-stocked refrigerator and pantry, birds and butterflies look to the flowers, foliage, berries, and seeds in your garden for their food. They also need fresh water for drinking and bathing. To really settle in and make your garden home, they also need cover in the form of trees and shrubs to feel safe and secure, as well as places to raise their families.

In this chapter, you'll learn more about the basic needs of songbirds, hummingbirds, and butterflies. Of course, you can't confine any of these fascinating

---

To feed birds from summer to early spring, plant a variety of shrubs that bear edible berries. Birds will eat the berries of some shrubs as soon as they ripen, and others will persist long into winter.

creatures to your backyard, but you can use these principles to create a yard and garden that will attract them and make them feel at home. In chapters 2 through 4, you'll find specific recommendations for attracting birds, hummingbirds, and butterflies, including lists of the plants they prefer.

FOOD

If birds and butterflies occasionally pass through your yard, but never seem to stay, it may be because you have been offering them only overnight accommodations — a passing meal, perhaps — instead of a varied, long-term food supply. To start designing plantings that attract songbirds, hummingbirds, and butterflies, it helps to know what they like to see on the menu. Flowers, fruits, seeds, and nuts from plantings of annuals, perennials, trees, shrubs, and vines — as well as weeds and grasses — are a good place to start. Garden insects and soil-dwellers such as earthworms, wireworms, beetles, and other organisms are also important menu items.

Hummingbirds and butterflies, of course, depend on flowers for nectar, but hummingbirds also eat a large number of insects, including weevils, gnats, aphids, and mosquitoes. In addition to flowers for nectar, adult butterflies need plants that will feed their larvae.

To encourage birds to stick around, you need to create a landscape that will allow them to find food daily. Birds that overwinter in your garden need to find food 365 days of the year. In fact, small birds like chickadees and nuthatches eat almost constantly during daylight hours, especially in the winter. Winter bird feeding is just part of the picture for overwintering species. Variety is also important. Many birds eat berries and other fruits that persist on trees and shrubs through winter. Woodpeckers and many songbirds scour tree trunks and branches for insect eggs and overwintering larvae.

Migratory songbirds need food for varying amounts of time: Warblers may pass through your yard and feast on insects for only a few weeks in spring and fall. Songbirds that come to your region to build nests and raise families need

---

TIPS FOR SUCCESS

Weeds aren't normally welcomed in gardens, but many weeds attract birds and butterflies in abundance because of their seeds, nectar, or the insects they attract. Set aside space for field species such as Queen-Anne's-lace, black-eyed Susans, native asters, goldenrods, milkweeds, and yarrows. Yellow-flowered *Impatiens pallida* and orange-flowered *I. capensis,* both commonly called jewelweed, are good plants for attracting hummingbirds. Both grow in moist to wet soil in shade.

This informal planting offers food to songbirds, hummingbirds, and butterflies. Coneflowers (Echinacea purpurea *and* Rudbeckia fulgida) *provide seeds for birds and nectar for butterflies. Both hummingbirds and butterflies visit the pink and white blooms of phlox* (Phlox carolina).

Cardinal flower (Lobelia cardinalis) *is a hummingbird favorite because of its spikes of scarlet trumpet-shaped blooms, borne in mid- to late summer.*

The leaves of Queen-Anne's-lace (Daucus carota) *are an important food for hungry swallowtail butterfly larvae. Consider growing it in a meadowlike planting, which will also attract a variety of seed-eating birds such as sparrows and juncos.*

New England asters (Aster novae-angliae) *provide a ready source of late summer to fall nectar for a variety of butterflies such as this orange sulphur, also called alfalfa sulphur. After the flowers fade, songbirds can feast on the seeds well into winter.*

Common winterberry (Ilex verticillata) *provides a bounty of winter berries for hungry birds and adds plenty of eye-catching color to the landscape in the process.*

food to feed their hungry broods for several months. Hummingbirds and butterflies need flowers for nectar from spring to fall in some areas.

Planning Food Sources. To create a landscape that provides birds and other wildlife with a guaranteed, year-round food supply, you need to plant an assortment of species that provides seeds, berries, nuts, or other food throughout the year. Planting a diverse selection helps ensure that a variety of food sources is always available. Feeding birds seeds and suet — in winter or all year — not only supplements what they find in your yard, it also makes it easy for you to enjoy watching them from indoors.

The best way to start planning a food supply for your guests is to take an inventory of what is already growing in your yard. Draw a rough map of your

Flowering dogwoods (Cornus florida) *produce berries in late summer and fall that attract more than 90 species of birds, including catbirds, mockingbirds, robins, thrushes, woodpeckers, bluebirds, and cardinals.*

property in a loose-leaf notebook. Take it outdoors and make notes about what plants are growing in your yard. (Use a field guide or garden book to identify plants you're not familiar with.) Also note what types of habitat you have available. Is your yard a mix of sun and shade, all sunny, or all shady?

Then use the lists in this book to determine which plants in your yard already provide food for birds and butterflies, and which do not. For example, 'Kwanzan' cherries are popular ornamental trees that bear large rounded clusters of double pink flowers in spring. But the flowers are sterile and do not yield berries for birds. Chokecherries *(Prunus virginiana)* and pin cherries *(Prunus pensylvanica)* not only have white spring flowers, they also produce berries relished by many birds, including bluebirds, mockingbirds, and catbirds. You may want to remove some plants that do not provide food in order to make room for ones that do.

Also note the season or seasons that the food is available. Making a chart or checklist in your notebook is a good way to do this. It's a good idea to assign different pages to different seasons, starting each page with the food-producing plants already growing in your yard. Then list plants you can add. Concentrate first on adding plants that provide food during seasons when nothing much is available in your yard. For example, if you have plenty of midsummer nectar sources for hummingbirds, but nothing in early summer or fall, you may want to plant columbines (*Aquilegia* spp.) and foxgloves (*Digitalis* spp.) for spring and early summer and annual salvias for fall. If butterfly larvae plants are in short supply, you might plant extra parsley and dill to feed the larvae of swallowtail butterflies. You will find a list of plants for butterfly larvae in chapter 4.

Keep your map and notes handy. That way you can keep records about plants to add to your landscape in one place. You may also want to add sections for jotting down notes about birds or other wildlife you see. Include some pockets so you can tuck in notes and clippings that provide ideas for improving your wildlife habitat.

Providing Safe Food. Organic gardening is another essential ingredient in any landscape that welcomes birds and butterflies. One reason is that organic gardens are teeming with insects and other organisms that birds enjoy. Since organic gardeners avoid chemical pesticides, fungicides, and fertilizers, birds are guaranteed a safe, chemical-free food supply and butterfly populations aren't affected.

Although any system that encourages insects may sound like a sure-fire recipe for disaster, birds will help control garden pests, along with annoying insects like gnats and mosquitoes. Many of the insects that thrive in an organic garden are beneficial: that is, they eat or parasitize pest insects and help keep populations in check. Other beneficial insects — honeybees most notably — pollinate flowers, which creates seeds and berries for birds to eat.

Good gardening practices are the cornerstones of organic gardening. Instead of waging war against pests and diseases with an arsenal of chemicals, organic gardeners seek to nudge the ecosystem into a healthy balance rather than bludgeon it into submission. Preventive techniques like building healthy soil are important first lines of defense against pests. (Healthy soil that is rich in organic matter is also rich in earthworms and other soil-dwellers, important sources of

Many annuals attract both hummingbirds and butterflies. This garden is planted with easy-to-grow cosmos, zinnias, and cleome.

food for birds.) Beneficial insects and animals are welcomed as allies. "Soft" controls, such as soaps, oils, and beneficial organisms like parasitic nematodes are used before stronger, plant-derived sprays and dusts, such as rotenone and sabadilla. Bt *(Bacillus thuringiensis)* is a toxin-producing pesticide that is generally considered safe; but keep in mind that Bt kills butterfly larvae along with larvae of pest insects like cabbage loopers. Avoid its use entirely, or use it only in very controlled applications in the vegetable garden. Avoid even organically acceptable plant-derived sprays for the same reason. (For more on organic gardening practices, see "Recommended Reading" on page 114.)

WATER

To most wildlife, the average suburban landscape looks like a desert. A yard covered in lawn grass with a few foundation shrubs simply doesn't provide many opportunities for bathing and drinking. Birds drink and bathe in the shallow water of ponds, streams, ditches, and puddles, as well as in birdbaths and garden pools. They'll even drink water that collects on the cupped foliage of plants like hostas after a rainstorm. Many species, including warblers, also "leaf bathe" by fluttering among the wet leaves of trees and shrubs after a rainstorm. In desert areas, birds depend on the leaves of succulent plants and the moisture contained in insects for their water needs. Many small desert species also leaf bathe.

Butterflies need water, too. Nectar and water found on flower petals provide much of what they drink. You'll also see them gathered on sandbars along a stream, on the muddy bank of a pond, or around a puddle of water, engaged in an activity called puddling, in which they drink water and take up mineral salts.

Fortunately, it's easy to add water sources to your garden. A birdbath is a good place to start. Most birds prefer a spot in a clearing, so position it in a sunny spot about 15 feet from trees and shrubs. That way, bathing birds can keep an eye out for predators and will have time to fly for cover. (Birds can't fly quickly with wet feathers.) Other species, including thrushes, prefer a ground-level spot under cover of dense shrubbery, so they can drop down and bathe unnoticed.

A natural depression in the ground that stays moist is natural-looking and a good alternative for a conventional birdbath. You can keep a moist spot filled with a garden hose even in dry weather. If you don't have an area that stays moist naturally, create one by digging out a shallow area, lining it with concrete, and keeping it filled with clean water.

Keep in mind that birds are wary of water that is more than 2 or 3 inches deep. Add a few good-sized stones that emerge from the water for smaller birds, butterflies, and beneficial insects to land on. Many species will also alight on a twig attached to the edge of a birdbath before entering the water to bathe. Whether you select a conventional birdbath or a ground-level pool, be sure it has rough edges so birds can walk up to the water without slipping.

It is important to remember that birds need *clean* water. For this reason, locate your birdbath within reach of a hose so it is easy to keep filled and clean.

A ready supply of clean water is an essential ingredient in any landscape that is designed to attract birds, butterflies, and other wildlife.

Providing Water in Winter

Providing water for birds in winter is relatively easy now that safe, economical birdbath heaters are readily available at wild bird centers, hardware stores, and garden centers. These heaters generally feature thermostats that keep water from freezing even in subzero temperatures while still conserving energy. Select a model that shuts off automatically when it runs out of water, and connect heaters only to properly grounded outlets. Be sure to clean the birdbath throughout the winter to provide safe water for drinking and bathing.

Empty and scrub out birdbaths every two to three days, especially in the summer, to prevent bacteria and algae from fouling the water. Never use cleaning chemicals to wash a birdbath, as they may endanger the very birds you are trying to attract.

Making Water More Attractive. Incorporating the sound and sight of moving water will increase the number of birds attracted to your water feature. Even a leaky bucket hung over a birdbath will increase its "bird appeal." Simply hang up a bucket or jug with a pin-sized hole and keep it filled with water. The sound of slowly dripping water will attract birds. A dripping hose can be used the same way.

Many wild bird centers, hardware stores, and nurseries sell a variety of small, recirculating fountains and sprayers that can be used in a birdbath or a small pond. Hummingbirds are particularly attracted to sprayers and will bathe by simply flying through the spray without landing at all.

For the serious bird gardener, a backyard pond or water garden is a possibility. Surrounded by natural-looking plantings and filled with water lilies and fish, it can be the perfect centerpiece for a bird garden. Be sure to design a shallow "beach" or other area for birds to bathe in with water that is no more than 3 inches deep. (Birds generally cannot reach the water in conventional water gardens, which have steep sides.) A fountain or small waterfall is easy to incorporate and will attract birds with the sound of moving water.

COVER AND NEST SITES

Both birds and butterflies need cover, or shelter, for protection from the elements as well as to escape predators. Birds also need secure places to roost at night and raise their young. Here again, the average suburban yard is a wasteland: a tree in the front yard surrounded by lawn may provide room for a single nest, but not much more.

Mixed plantings of trees, shrubs, vines, perennials, annuals, and grasses provide ideal cover and many options for nest sites for a wide variety of birds. The best plants to choose also provide food — seeds, nuts, berries, nectar. Plants with densely branching or suckering habits are excellent because they produce thick

Dense plantings of trees and shrubs — both deciduous and evergreen — provide nest sites and protection from winter winds. This planting features kousa dogwood (Cornus kousa), with its raspberry-like fruit, and a low-growing cultivar of Canada hemlock (Tsuga canadensis).

Evergreens such as American holly (Ilex opaca) that provide wind protection, safe nest sites, and winter berries are especially valuable wildlife plants.

cover. For nest sites, thorns are a plus, because they provide extra predator protection. For this reason, shrub roses and hawthorns (*Crataegus* spp.) are excellent choices.

Needle- and broad-leaved evergreen trees and shrubs, such as white pines, arborvitae, spruce, junipers, cedars, and hollies, provide essential winter protection as well as food. (Birds eat the seeds, berries, and sap of many of these plants.) Different species of birds need different types of cover, however. Species like meadowlarks, field sparrows, and bobolinks prefer grassy meadow or prairie habitat for feeding and nesting.

ARRANGING COVER PLANTS

The way you arrange the plants in your yard will have an effect on how appealing it is to birds, butterflies, and other wildlife. Once again, variety is the key to success — both in the number of different plants you select and in the types of habitats you create.

To determine what the best arrangement is for your yard, turn to the rough map you made. Draw arrows to indicate the prevailing winter winds in your area — winds from the northwest are common throughout the country; areas along the East Coast may have winds that come from the east, off the Atlantic, that are most troublesome in winter. Ideally, plantings should provide protection from prevailing winds, especially in the winter. Butterflies also benefit from wind protection in summer, so they aren't buffeted about by breezes.

Rows of evergreens or mixed plantings of evergreens and tall deciduous trees are very effective for blocking wind. If the prevailing winter winds in your region come from the northwest, plant them along the north and west sides of your yard. A row of evergreens will work, but a mixed planting in a free-form shape is more natural looking. A fifty-fifty mix of deciduous and evergreen species is ideal.

To create a really effective barrier that is also rich in food and nest sites, mix in smaller trees and shrubs in layers along the front (leeward) side. Small-fruited crabapples, shrub roses, serviceberries (*Amelanchier* spp.), and deciduous hollies are all ideal for planting along a windbreak. Add beds of perennials and annuals in front that provide seeds and nectar. Or plant a large sunny area with meadow or prairie plants.

Every yard presents opportunities for creating different types of habitats that welcome winged wildlife. The more kinds of plantings you have, the more varied wildlife your yard will attract. You can underplant trees with shade-loving plants, fill a wet area with bog plants, and plant a sunny garden designed to attract hummingbirds, butterflies, and seed-eating birds. Look at the conditions that prevail in your yard and your region for ideas. Nature centers, botanical gardens, and wild bird centers have books and other information about plants and plant communities that are native to your region. Here are some ideas to consider.

Shade Plantings. Underplanting a wooded lot with food-rich species is an ideal way to create a bird-friendly landscape. Woodland edges are especially rich habitats for both birds and butterflies, because they feature both sun and shade plants and offer plenty of cover. Adding berried shrubs to an existing shade garden is another option. Even a yard that has only a few shade trees underplanted with lawn can be made more hospitable for birds. (Cutting down on lawn maintenance is an added benefit!) Remove the grass under one or more trees. Then underplant with a mix of shade-tolerant shrubs and small trees to create shady islands of plants. Add shade-loving perennials, ground covers, wildflowers, and annuals.

Shrubs and trees recommended for shady sites include dogwoods, azaleas and rhododendrons, shade-tolerant viburnums, hollies (*Ilex* spp.), blueberries (*Vaccinium* spp.), Oregon grape holly (*Mahonia aquifolium*), and spicebush (*Lindera benzoin*). Crabapples (*Malus* spp.) and hawthorns (*Crataegus* spp.) can be planted in clearings and along woodland edges. Perennials include hostas, violets, columbines, and wild strawberries (*Fragaria virginiana*). Northern sea oats (*Chasmanthium latifolium*) is a shade-tolerant ornamental grass.

TIPS FOR SUCCESS

Many birds depend on leaf litter, especially in wooded areas, so don't routinely rake it out of beds, borders, shade gardens, or wooded areas. Decomposing leaves return essential organic matter to the soil, but for birds leaf litter also contains an abundance of food. Birds such as thrushes, towhees, and fox sparrows hunt through it to find insects, fallen seeds, and berries to eat. The larvae of many insects overwinter in leaf litter — including some butterfly species: raking it up not only eliminates a winter food source, it also diminishes summer populations.

Shady areas can be made attractive to many songbirds by adding shrubs as well as perennials such as hostas and magic lilies (Lycoris squamigera).

Sun Plantings. A bounty of sun-loving plants will attract songbirds, humming-birds, and butterflies, and these plants can be incorporated into a landscape in many ways. Flower beds and borders are an obvious choice for sunny sites. Plant them around a patio or birdbath, along a windbreak planting of trees and shrubs, or all along the back boundary of your yard. To add variety and all-season interest, try mixing in small trees and shrubs.

For a more natural look, consider meadow or prairielike plantings. The best way to turn a small patch of lawn into meadow or prairie is to start with flower transplants, either homegrown or store-bought. For larger areas, seed is the only economical way to go.

Select a mix of wildflowers and native grasses that has been developed for

Meadow plantings attract plenty of wildlife, including seed-eating birds and butterflies seeking nectar and host plants for their larvae. Birds such as field sparrows will nest among the tall grasses and wildflowers.

Cannas and scarlet sage are ideal plants for attracting hummingbirds. This garden also features other annuals that will provide seeds for songbirds.

your region of the country. Avoid generic mixes developed for the entire country or "instant" meadow mixes, which generally contain mostly annuals. (See "Flowers and Grasses for a Bird Garden" on page 52 for a list of species to consider planting.)

To plant transplants or sow seeds, start by preparing the soil in midsummer. First mark out the area you plan to plant, mow it as close as possible, then till it under. Then either wait two weeks, till shallowly again to kill newly sprouted weeds, and repeat the tilling process two or three more times to control weeds; or lay four layers of newpaper on the ground and spread about an inch of mature compost on top.

Plant transplants in fall or early spring — whenever you commonly plant perennials. Use a bulb planter or a trowel to dig holes for the plants. Arrange the plants in a random pattern, clumping groups of the same plants together in some areas. Water and then mulch the plants with organic mulch — up to but not touching the stems — to control weeds.

To seed a meadow, in Zone 3 and south, plan to have the soil ready to sow one month before the first frost of fall. Or prepare the soil in midsummer and sow in early spring the following year, as soon as you can work the soil. Top-dress with a 1/4-inch layer of topsoil or finely screened compost, and water it well.

Cut your new meadow annually in winter or very early spring; you may need to use a string trimmer first, if it's quite high, then mow.

GROWING WITH YOUR DESIGN

Trying to transform a barren landscape into a haven for birds and butterflies overnight is an easy way to become frustrated. Instead of trying to replant everything at once, plan on making gradual changes over the course of several planting seasons. Use the notes you have made about food plants you have, and ones you want to plant, as a guide. You may also want to consult a book on garden design and draw up a master plan to follow over the years.

Identify one or two areas to concentrate on for the first year. If you already have a barrier of evergreens along the northwest side of your property, for example, you might want to spend your time and energy adding trees and shrubs in front of it that will provide additional cover and food. If you have a single tree in the front yard, you could consider adding more trees and underplanting with berry-producing shrubs and ground covers.

Plan to add plants gradually as your budget and time allow. Buy the largest plants you can afford, and only as many as you can care for at one time. Proper soil preparation, watering, mulching, and weeding are all essential to getting plants off to a good start. You'll be rewarded with much larger, healthier plants if you lavish care on a few specimens at a time instead of providing the bare minimum for a host of plants. For large, expensive trees, you may consider having a nursery do the planting. Not only do they handle the sweat and strain of planting, they also have equipment to handle larger specimens with the least amount of stress on the plant. Most nurseries offer a replacement guarantee for trees and shrubs they plant; some guarantee even those they don't plant.

Over time, you'll find that growing a garden that welcomes winged wildlife provides benefits for people as well as birds. The plants that attract songbirds, hummingbirds, and butterflies have a rich natural beauty, and a garden designed to be full of flowers and fruits — as well as flashing feathers and glittering wings — has unmatched appeal. Natural insect control, low maintenance, increased property value, and energy conservation from windbreak plantings are other, less obvious benefits of a well-planned wildlife garden.

Fine-tuning your bird garden can become a life-long pursuit, and watching the birds that visit can become an entertaining hobby. You may want to keep notes on the birds you see, behaviors you observe, and the plants they visit most often. Over the years, you will undoubtedly find new trees, shrubs, vines, perennials, and annuals to add, or new combinations of plants to try, that will improve the habitats you've created. Trees and shrubs will grow larger, bear more fruit, and provide opportunities for underplanting with shade-tolerant species. Enjoy your changing landscape and the wildlife that it attracts.

Bleeding heart (Dicentra eximia) *blooms in spring and summer and will attract butterflies such as this tiger swallowtail as well as hummingbirds.*

CHAPTER 2:
CREATING A BIRD GARDEN

Planting trees, shrubs, vines, and flowers that appeal to birds is the most important step you can take toward creating a backyard bird haven. Adding a source of fresh, clean water is a second essential step. Chapter 1 covered the basics of how to design a bird garden and arrange the plants in it. This chapter features the plants that attract birds, from towering evergreens and deciduous trees to shrubs, annuals, and perennials.

Fortunately, birds and gardeners are attracted to many of the same plants, or at least to similar ones. In fact, the best species for birds include many beloved garden plants, including dogwoods, crabapples, and viburnums. As a result, it is an easy matter to create an attractive garden that appeals to birds and people alike.

Many annuals and perennials, such as purple coneflowers (Echinacea purpurea), *produce a bounty of seeds that will feed birds well into winter.*

Keep in mind, however, that birds and gardeners make their plant choices for entirely different reasons. While a gardener plants dogwoods and crabapples for their gorgeous spring flowers, birds have their own plans for these trees. To them, the flowers provide an ideal hunting ground for insects, and the fruit offers essential food in fall and winter. Viburnums are another case in point. Cultivated forms with showy, fragrant snowball-like blooms are popular garden plants, but birds pass right by them, because the flowers are sterile and don't yield berries. For a bird garden, viburnums with smaller, but fertile, flowers and the added bonus of showy fall fruit are the best choice.

Birds also use plants with evergreen foliage for winter cover, and dense, twiggy growth to provide safe nesting sites and protection from predators. Mixed shrub borders, shade plantings, and even semiwild hedgerows are perfect ways to incorporate these needs into an attractive landscape that will attract birds. (See "Arranging Cover Plants" on page 17 for more ideas on how to incorporate bird-attracting plants into your yard.)

In this chapter, you'll find information on some of the best plants for a bird garden. Before you decide what to plant, though, do some local research on the recommended plants for your area. Nature centers, botanical gardens, wild bird centers, and your local library or extension service office have materials available on trees, shrubs, vines, and flowers that are adapted to your climate and attractive to birds in your region. They also have access to information on the types of habitats that are typically found in your region. You also may find experts at a local nursery or garden center. Many gardeners interested in landscaping for wildlife plant only indigenous species. You can use field guides to identify plants that are native to your area.

FEEDING THE BIRDS

Bird feeding is a terrific hobby that you can enjoy year-round. But for birds, the seed, suet, and other treats you put out during the winter months can be a lifesaver. Many homeowners feed in summer, too, because it allows them to watch birds from indoors all year. There's nothing quite like watching parent birds introduce their latest batch of babies to your feeders.

A basic seed mix of black-oil sunflower, white proso millet, and safflower seed

To create a garden that attracts songbirds like this yellow warbler, plant an assortment of trees, shrubs, and vines that offer safe nesting sites and winter cover.

will attract a wide variety of birds that routinely visit feeders. If you like, you can add specialty items such as niger thistle, which attracts goldfinches, and fine or medium cracked corn, which appeals to species like jays and white-throated sparrows. Wild bird centers will be able to tell you which local species are attracted to the different types of seed mixes they sell.

To attract the widest variety of birds, use several models of feeders and provide food at various heights. Low platforms attract ground-eating species like juncos and mourning doves and keep the seed dry during inclement weather. You can also spread seed on rocks or even right on the ground. Position feeders in sheltered spots that you can see easily from indoors.

Suet feeders attract woodpeckers, as well as nuthatches, chickadees, and Carolina wrens. Avoid using suet when daytime temperatures are above 70°F, because it can turn rancid. You can buy commercial suet mixes, including ones designed for summer feeding, or you can buy chunks of beef suet at the butcher.

Summer feeding has its own rewards. With oranges, bananas, raisins, and apples, you can lure orioles, tanagers, robins, and mockingbirds to your feeders. Cut the fruit in half and hang it on an opened coat hanger, stick it on a tree branch, or fasten it to your feeder. Nectar feeders will attract hummingbirds and orioles in addition to hummingbirds. For more on them, see chapter 3.

Ideally, maintain two or more feeding areas in different parts of your yard — one out in the lawn near a group of evergreens, for example, and another in a shade garden or wooded area. Try to be as consistent as possible in keeping feeders filled: the birds that visit your feeders will come to depend on them daily.

TIPS FOR SUCCESS

If you provide backyard birds with a conventional birdbath, adding a fountain or sprayer will add the sight and sound of moving water and attract even more birds. A garden pond that has a shallow end for bathing and a small fountain or waterfall will attract yet more birds, along with dragonflies, frogs, toads, and other creatures. While you're at it, why not add a bog garden at one end, too? You may see robins, phoebes, or barn swallows come and gather mud to make their nests.

NEST BOXES AND OTHER FEATURES FOR BIRDS

In addition to feeding birds and growing plants that provide food and cover, there are other steps you can take to make your yard attractive to birds. Consider these options:

Provide Nest Boxes and Platforms. Putting up nest boxes is another way to attract birds to your yard. Species that use them include bluebirds, tree swallows, wrens, purple martins, tufted titmice, chickadees, nuthatches, and woodpeckers. Platforms or nesting shelves will attract species such as robins, barn swallows, and phoebes. Put up different types of boxes and hang them in a variety of habitats to attract many species of birds. You can also offer nesting materials, if you like. Hang an old suet feeder or wire basket and fill it with dog or cat hair, short strips of cotton fabric, excelsior, or short (8 inches or less) lengths of string or yarn. Stick to natural, biodegradable materials.

Locate birdbaths or other water features where they are easy to fill and clean. A site within view of a window will let you enjoy visitors all year.

Put Up Roosting Boxes. Many small birds such as chickadees huddle together at night in winter to conserve heat. Specially designed roosting boxes are available at wild bird centers. These feature a hole near the bottom, which prevents heat from escaping, and perches designed so birds don't sit directly over one another. Some models can be turned over and converted to conventional bird houses for summer.

Save a Snag. People usually consider dead and dying trees, called snags, eyesores, but many birds see them as home. So, before you remove a tree, stop to consider that you are taking down real estate that woodpeckers and many other

Berries that persist on trees and shrubs through the winter provide important food for a variety of birds like this robin, as well as bluebirds, mockingbirds, catbirds, and waxwings.

birds adore. Woodpeckers are the major engineers that hollow out nesting cavities in dead trees, but many other species enjoy the cavities they hollow out, including chickadees, nuthatches, wrens, tree swallows, brown creepers, great crested flycatchers, and bluebirds. Birds will also nest in the hollow limbs of venerable old trees like oaks. Dead trees also provide ideal hunting grounds for insects, and many birds use them simply to perch and watch over their territory. The ideal snag is at least 6 inches in diameter and more than 15 feet tall. Leaving a dead tree isn't an option for everyone, but if you can, leave one in your garden. If you want to dress up a dead tree, use it as a trellis. Trumpet vine *(Campsis radicans)* will cover up even a large snag and attract hummingbirds in the process. Dedicated backyard wildlife enthusiasts have even erected snags in their yards in order to enjoy the birds they attract.

Make a Dust Bath. Water isn't the only thing that birds bathe in. Many small songbirds visit dry, dusty sites and "bathe" in them to control parasites. You can add a dust bath to your bird garden by pulverizing the soil in a $1\frac{1}{2}$- to 2-foot-diameter area. Either use a garden fork to dig the soil to between 6 and 8 inches and a hoe to pulverize it, or till the area repeatedly. To pulverize the soil most effectively, work it when it is dry.

TREES FOR A BIRD GARDEN

Trees are the backbone of a landscape designed to attract birds. Not only do they produce edible seeds and nuts, they also provide essential hunting grounds for insect eaters. Many birds search the flowers and foliage of trees and eat the insects that they find there. Flycatchers, phoebes, kingbirds, and other species make forays from tree branches to catch nearby flying insects. Trees also provide winter cover, nest sites, and places to hide from predators.

■ *Abies* spp. / Firs

DESCRIPTION: Distinctive and popular, these handsome, densely branched evergreens provide important cover and plentiful seeds for a variety of species. They are pyramidal to columnar in habit and grow slowly to heights of 40 to

100 feet, depending on the species. The seeds are contained in upright cones that appear in summer. In late fall, when they reach maturity, the cones open to scatter seeds that are relished by many kinds of birds. Firs are best suited to regions with cool, humid conditions like those of their mountainous native habitats. White fir *(Abies concolor)*, nikko fir *(A. homolepis)*, and noble fir *(A. procera)* are all good choices. Balsam fir *(A. balsamea)* and Fraser fir *(A. fraseri)* are also popular.

BIRDS ATTRACTED: Many species, including towhees, nuthatches, grosbeaks, chickadees, crossbills, and jays. Blue and sharp-tailed grouse eat the flat needles.

CULTURE: Grow firs in moist, well-drained, acid soil. They tolerate light shade, but a site in full sun is best. Mulch the soil with leaves, shredded bark, or wood chips to keep the roots cool and the soil moist. Zones 4–7, depending on the species.

■ *Acer* spp. / Maples

DESCRIPTION: Maples produce a bounty of summer seeds for birds, along with nest sites and cover. Birds also hunt for insects among the early spring flowers and summer foliage. These broad-spreading trees have lobed leaves and range in height from 25 to 100 feet at maturity. There are many good species to choose from. Amur maple *(Acer ginnala)* is a good choice for small gardens; red maple *(A. rubrum)* and sugar maple *(A. saccharum)* are large trees for large spaces. Boxelder *(A. negundo)* is considered a weed tree in some parts of the country, but produces abundant crops of seeds and is a good choice in the Great Plains and Southwest. Boxelder is dioecious, so be sure to buy male and female trees to obtain seeds. Japanese maple *(A. palmatum)* is a fine plant for sites in dappled shade.

BIRDS ATTRACTED: Cardinals, grosbeaks, and purple finches eat the seeds. Chickadees, nuthatches, warblers, and other species hunt for insects in the bark and among the leaves and flowers.

CULTURE: In general, maples grow best in rich, moist, well-drained soil and will grow in full sun to half-shade. They require irrigation in areas that receive less than 30 inches of rainfall per year. Zones 3–9, depending on the species.

Saskatoon serviceberry (Amelanchier alnifolia) *produces clusters of tiny white flowers followed by round purple-black berries.*

- *Amelanchier* **spp. / Serviceberries**

DESCRIPTION: Also called shadbush, shadblow, and juneberry, these small, deciduous trees produce clouds of tiny white flowers in spring. The flowers are followed by small purplish fruit that attracts both birds and humans. Many species make ideal additions to bird gardens and are especially effective planted on the edges of woodlands, in shrub borders, and along streams and ponds. Plants range in size from 10 to 20 feet. Downy serviceberry *(A. arborea),* saskatoon serviceberry *(A. alnifolia),* and Allegheny serviceberry *(A. laevis)* are good choices. Shadblow serviceberry *(A. canadensis)* is a shrubby, 6- to 20-foot species that spreads by suckers. Running serviceberry *(A. stolonifera)* is a stoloniferous shrub that forms thickets.

BIRDS ATTRACTED: Many species eat the berries, including bluebirds, catbirds, grosbeaks, jays, mockingbirds, robins, thrushes, woodpeckers, towhees, orioles, tanagers, and cedar waxwings. The spring flowers also attract insects that many birds appreciate.

CULTURE: Serviceberries will grow in ordinary garden soil but prefer moist, well-drained, acid conditions. They tolerate partial shade. Mulch to keep the soil moist. Water during very dry spells. Zones 4–8, depending on the species.

■ *Celtis* spp. / Hackberries

DESCRIPTION: Although often overlooked as ornamentals, hackberries make valuable additions to any bird garden because of their small ($1/3$ inch) blackish purple fruit. They are ideal trees to plant in difficult sites because they tolerate a wide range of soil conditions, as well as air pollution. Use these large, 40- to 60-foot trees as background plants, behind shrub borders, or to provide shade on a tough site. Common hackberry *(Celtis occidentalis)* and sugar hackberry *(C. laevigata)* are two good choices.

BIRDS ATTRACTED: Bluebirds, fox sparrows, flickers and woodpeckers, cardinals, mockingbirds, thrashers, thrushes, quail, phoebes, towhees, and titmice are among the birds that eat the berries. Many species also nest in the branches.

CULTURE: Hackberries tolerate acid or alkaline soil that ranges from somewhat wet to very dry, although they do best in rich, moist soil. Plant them in full sun.

■ *Cornus* spp. / Dogwoods

DESCRIPTION: Dogwoods are excellent plants for a bird garden because of their tasty berries that provide food in summer, fall, and winter. All bear spring flowers with showy white, or sometimes pink, bracts. The flowers are followed by bright fruit and stunning fall color, making these trees outstanding specimen plants or lovely additions to tree and shrub borders. Flowering dogwood *(C. florida)* is a beloved ornamental with clusters of shiny red berries in fall (see photo on page 9). Kousa or Japanese dogwood *(Cornus kousa)* bears blooms slightly later and has red, raspberry-like fruits. Both are small trees ranging from 20 to 30 feet. Pacific dogwood *(Cornus nuttalli)* is a large tree (to 75 feet) with red or orange summer-to-fall fruits. It is best grown in the Pacific Northwest. (For information on shrubby dogwoods, see "*Cornus* spp." on page 45.)

Kousa dogwood (Cornus kousa) *features showy, raspberry-like fruit on long stalks.*

BIRDS ATTRACTED: More than 90 species of birds eat dogwood berries, including catbirds, mockingbirds, robins, thrushes, woodpeckers, vireos, white-throated sparrows, song sparrows, bluebirds, cardinals, and kingbirds. Many warblers and other birds also hunt for insects among dogwood branches and in the furrows of the bark.

CULTURE: Dogwoods grow well in most good garden soils, but prefer well-drained, acid soil that is rich in organic matter. Mulch to keep the soil moist and cool. Partial shade is ideal, although dogwoods will tolerate full sun. Zones 5–9, depending on the species; *C. nuttalli* is hardy in Zones 7–9.

■ *Crataegus* spp. / Hawthorns

DESCRIPTION: These small trees produce clusters of white spring flowers followed by clusters of small berries that attract a number of birds. Their branches are generally armed with stout, sharp thorns, which provide excellent protection for nesting birds. Cockspur hawthorn (*Crataegus crus-galli*) and Lavalle hawthorn (*C. × lavallei*) bear ½-inch fruit; Washington hawthorn (*C. phaeonpyrum*) is an especially good choice because of its smaller, ¼-inch fruits, which can be eaten by more species. Hummingbirds also visit its flowers. Use these plants for barrier plantings, as well as tree and shrub borders.

BIRDS ATTRACTED: Jays, mockingbirds, robins, and grosbeaks are among the birds that eat hawthorn berries. Mourning doves and cardinals are two of the species that nest among the thorny branches. Many species also search for insects among the leaves and flowers.

CULTURE: Hawthorns grow well in ordinary to poor garden soil. They are especially suited for alkaline soil and withstand drought and harsh weather. Plant in full sun. Avoid planting them near walkways because of their thorns; prune off branches or thorns that might pose a hazard for garden visitors. Zones 3–9, depending on the species.

■ *Ilex* spp. / Hollies

DESCRIPTION: The round, red, pea-sized berries of hollies provide important fall to early spring food for many kinds of birds. Trees in this genus, which range from 20 to 50 feet in height, also provide important cover because of their glossy, evergreen leaves. Use hollies as specimen plants and in tree and shrub borders. American holly (*Ilex opaca*, see photo on page 16) and longstalk holly (*I. pedunculosa*) are good choices. English holly (*I. aquifolium*) is a good choice south of Zone 7, although it does not grow well in areas with hot, dry summers. (For information on shrub hollies, see "*Ilex* spp." on page 45.)

BIRDS ATTRACTED: Bluebirds, robins, waxwings, catbirds, and mockingbirds are among the species that enjoy the berries, which generally last well into winter.

CULTURE: Plant hollies in partial shade in acid, loamy soil that is well drained. Protect plants from wind. Spring planting of balled-and-burlapped or container-grown plants is recommended. Be sure to plant both male and female plants of any species you grow to ensure berries; one male will pollinate three female plants. Zones 5–9.

Western or California juniper (Juniperus occidentalis) *is a shrub or small tree that bears abundant crops of berries.*

■ *Juniperus* spp. / Junipers

DESCRIPTION: The round, blue, berrylike fruits of many junipers and the dense, evergreen branches covered with scalelike needles attract a variety of birds. Although many shrub-sized junipers are available, trees in this genus are preferable because they provide nest sites and winter cover. Eastern red cedar *(Juniperus virginiana)* and Rocky Mountain juniper or Western red cedar *(J. scopulorum)* are both good choices that range from 40 to 75 feet in height.

BIRDS ATTRACTED: The berries provide important winter food for a variety of species, including bluebirds, catbirds, crossbills, purple finches, grosbeaks, jays, mockingbirds, quail, and thrushes. Native sparrows, robins, and mockingbirds often nest in junipers.

CULTURE: Plant junipers in full sun in a site with well-drained soil. They will grow in evenly moist, well-drained soils and also endure dry, rocky sites as well as wind and drought. Zones 3–10, depending on the species.

■ *Malus* spp. / Crabapple, apples

DESCRIPTION: Crabapples produce a glorious spring display of white or pink flowers followed by berries savored by a variety of birds. These small round-headed trees, which range from 15 to 30 feet in height, also offer secure nest sites. Many species hunt for insects among the leaves and branches of both crabapples and apples. Hummingbirds visit the flowers. The best crabapples for feeding birds bear small fruit that persists on the trees into winter. See "Small-Fruited Crabapples" below for a list of species and cultivars to consider.

BIRDS ATTRACTED: Woodpeckers and flickers, robins, mockingbirds, catbirds, and grosbeaks all eat crabapples.

CULTURE: Grow crabapples in moist, well-drained soil and full sun. They tolerate acid to somewhat alkaline soils. Zones 3 or 4–8, depending on the species.

Small-Fruited Crabapples

Many popular crabapples feature fruit that is far too large for birds to fit in their mouths. You can provide a veritable feast that lasts well into winter by planting cultivars that bear fruit under ½ inch in diameter. (Birds generally wait to eat the fruit until it has been softened by winter freezes.) The following crabapples all bear fruit smaller than that — from ¼ to ⅓ inch in diameter — that even small birds can enjoy with ease. In addition, all the cultivars listed are also disease-resistant.

Species crabapples include carmine crabapple *Malus × atrosanguinea,* Japanese flowering crabapple *Malus floribunda,* tea crabapple *Malus hupehensis,* and Sargent crabapple *Malus sargentii.*

Cultivars include 'Autumn Glory', 'Autumn Treasure', 'Donald Wyman', 'Fiesta', 'Firebelle', 'Firebrand', 'Fireburst', 'Golden Dream', 'Cornell', 'Katherine', 'Little Troll', 'Matador', 'Molten Lava', 'Pagoda', 'Peter Pan', 'Sea Foam', 'Sinai Fire', 'Wildfire', 'Woven Gold', and 'Zumirang'.

Sargent crabapple (Malus sargentii) *is a small tree that produces clouds of white flowers in late spring followed by small dark red berries.*

- ### *Morus* spp. / Mulberries

DESCRIPTION: Mulberries are often first on the list of undesirable weed trees, but that's not where birds would rank them. The succulent purple-black berries, which are borne only on female trees, provide a bounty of summer food for birds and a variety of other wild creatures — including box turtles. They range from 30 to 50 feet in height and also offer safe cover and nest sites. Use them in wild areas, hedgerows, or as background plants. Common mulberry *(Morus alba)*, red mulberry *(M. rubra)*, and Texas mulberry *(M. microphylla)* are species to look for. Be sure to select a fruiting, female plant, not one of the new, male, nonfruiting cultivars.

BIRDS ATTRACTED: Nearly 60 species of birds relish mulberries, including scarlet tanagers, orioles, cardinals, phainopepla, woodpeckers, bluebirds, and waxwings.

CULTURE: Grow mulberries in almost any soil in full sun. Zones 4–9, depending on the species.

Norway spruce (Picea abies) *bears 6-inch-long cones that provide seeds for many birds in winter. The dense branches offer winter cover as well.*

■ *Picea* spp. / Spruces

DESCRIPTION: Spruces are pyramidal evergreens that provide important winter cover as well as edible seeds. Grouse eat the needles. Spruce trees range from 60 to over 100 feet in height. Their sharp needles and densely branching habit make them ideal nest sites. Use these large plants as windbreaks, specimens, or as backdrops for other shrubs and trees. Norway spruce *(Picea abies)*, Serbian spruce *(P. omorika)*, and Colorado spruce *(P. pungens)* are three popular species.

BIRDS ATTRACTED: Nuthatches, crossbills, chickadees, pine siskins, and grosbeaks all eat spruce seeds.

CULTURE: Plant spruces in full sun to light shade. They will tolerate a range of soils, but require evenly moist conditions. Avoid soil that is too dry or too wet. Also avoid exposed sites where they will be subjected to drying winds. Zones 2–7, depending on the species.

■ *Pinus* spp. / Pines

DESCRIPTION: These magnificent evergreens provide cover, winter protection, and nest sites, as well as edible seeds and sap. Several species of grouse, as well as wild turkeys, eat the needles. Most are large trees, from 60 to 100 feet at maturity. Dwarf and slow-growing cultivars of many species are available. There are

---

More Trees for Birds

In addition to the trees described in this chapter, the following are also recommended for attracting birds because of the berries, seeds, or nuts they provide, or because of their value as cover. Plants marked with a symbol (❂) tolerate partial shade.

Evergreen trees
Chamaecyparis spp. Cedars.
Pseudotsuga menziesii. Douglas fir.
Thuja occidentalis. American arborvitae.
Tsuga. Hemlock.
    Especially *T. canadensis*
    and *T. caroliniana.*

Deciduous trees
Alnus spp. Alders.
    Especially *A. glutinosa.* ❂
Betula spp. Birches.
    Especially *B. lenta, B. papyrifera,*
    B. occidentalis, and *B. populifolia.*

Carya spp. Hickories.
Corylus spp. Hazlenuts, filberts. ❂
Elaeagnus spp. Russian olives.
    Especially *E. angustifolia, E. multiflora,*
    and *E. umbellata.* (Note: These can be
    weedy and have been declared noxious
    weeds in some states.)
Fagus spp. Beeches. ❂
Fraxinus spp. Ashes.
Liriodendron tulipifera. Tulip tree.
Nyssa sylvatica. Black gum. ❂
Platanus spp. Sycamores.
Populus spp. Poplars or cottonwoods.
Sorbus spp. Mountain ashes.

White pine (Pinus strobus) *can be used in windbreaks, and it also provides food and nest sites for a variety of species.*

species for gardens in every part of the country, including eastern white pine *(P. strobus)*, jack pine *(P. banksiana)*, and red pine *(P. resinosa)* for the Midwest and East. Longleaf and loblolly pines *(P. palustris* and *P. taeda)* are suitable for the Southeast. For prairie states west to the Pacific, species include Lodgepole pine *(P. contorta)*, limber pine *(P. flexilis)*, ponderosa pine *(P. ponderosa)*, and Mexican pinyon *(P. cembroides)*.

BIRDS ATTRACTED: Many species, including grosbeaks, jays, nuthatches, pine siskins, titmice, towhees, woodpeckers, crossbills, and Clark's nutcrackers eat the seeds.

CULTURE: Most pines grow well in light to average, well-drained soil and full sun. Some species tolerate dry soil. Use these evergreens to create windbreaks to block prevailing winter winds. They also make fine specimen trees. Zones 2–10, depending on the species.

■ *Prunus* spp. / Cherries

DESCRIPTION: As anyone who raises sweet cherries *(Prunus avium)* or tart cherries *(P. cerasus)* for pies and jellies knows, birds relish these glossy, round, red fruits. In addition to cultivated cherries, they also gobble up the summer fruit of a variety of wild cherries, including pin cherry *(P. pensylvanica)*, wild black cherry *(P. serotina)*, and chokecherry *(P. virginiana)*. In desert and mountain regions, bitter cherry *(P. emarginata)* and western chokecherry *(P. virginiana* var. *demissa)* make good additions to bird gardens. Sand cherry *(P. besseyi)* is a suckering shrub that reaches 6 feet and bears purple-black fruit. In general, cherries are small trees, from 15 to 40 feet in height, that are effective in shrub borders and hedgerows.

BIRDS ATTRACTED: More than 80 species of birds eat cherries, including robins, bluebirds, woodpeckers, catbirds, thrushes, cardinals, blackbirds, tanagers, jays, and orioles.

CULTURE: Plant cherries in full sun and evenly moist, well-drained soil. Mulch them to keep the soil cool and moist, and water deeply during periods of drought. Zones 5–10, depending on the species.

- *Quercus* spp. / Oaks

DESCRIPTION: Oaks are majestic trees that produce acorns and also provide nesting sites. There are about 450 species of oaks, ranging from mid-sized 40- or 50-foot trees to giants that exceed 100 feet. The region you live in is the best indicator of which species to plant. For eastern gardens, white oak *(Quercus alba)*, scarlet oak *(Q. coccinea)*, bur oak *(Q. macrocarpa)*, and pin oak *(Q. palustris)* are nice choices. Southeastern gardeners can grow laurel oak *(Q. laurifolia)*, blackjack oak *(Q. marilandica)*, willow oak *(Q. phellos)*, and live oak *(Q. virginiana)*. Bur oak *(Q. macrocarpa)* is a good selection for the Great Plains, as are shingle oak *(Q. imbricaria)* and blackjack oak *(Q. marilandica)*. Gardeners in western regions can consider Gambel oak *(Q. gambeli)* and Rocky Mountain white oak *(Q. utahensis)*. In Zones 8 and warmer along the Pacific coast, canyon live oak *(Q. chrysolepis)*, California black oak *(Q. kelloggii)*, and valley oak *(Q. lobata)* are the best options.

BIRDS ATTRACTED: Jays are major acorn consumers, but many other birds will also eat them, including chickadees, grouse, bobwhites and quail, grosbeaks, and cardinals. Many of these species also hunt for insects among the branches. In western states, acorn woodpeckers collect and store vast quantities of the nuts.

CULTURE: Oaks grow best in full sun, although most will tolerate some partial shade. Rich, deep soil is ideal. Mulch oak trees, but avoid grade changes, trenching, and soil compaction in the root zone, which can kill them. Transplanting can be tricky, but fortunately researchers have recently developed new techniques for growing oaks in containers, and more species can be successfully transplanted than ever before. Zones 4–10, depending on the species.

SHRUBS AND BRAMBLES FOR A BIRD GARDEN

Even gardeners who don't have space for more than one full-size tree on their property can find room for an assortment of smaller shrubs or a thicket of bramble fruit. For best results, plant several different shrubs — either individually or in masses — and combine them with larger trees to create dense plantings that provide cover as well as food. You can also underplant existing trees with berry-producing shrubs to create a food-rich woodland or shade planting. Shrubs also work well when incorporated into perennial gardens.

- *Cornus* spp. / Dogwoods

DESCRIPTION: Shrubby dogwoods bear spring flowers and a wealth of berries relished by many species of birds. They make excellent additions to gardens in eastern states and in the Plains states. These species are shrubs to small trees and range in height from 6 to 25 feet. Use them in tree and shrub borders, massed along foundations, or in naturalized areas. Species to plant include Tatarian dogwood *(Cornus alba),* cornelian cherry dogwood *(C. mas),* gray dogwood *(C. racemosa),* pagoda dogwood *(C. alternifolia),* rough-leaved dogwood *(C. asperifolia),* red osier dogwood *(C. sericea),* and round-leaved dogwood *(C. rugosa).* (For information on tree dogwoods, see "*Cornus* spp." on page 34.)

BIRDS ATTRACTED: More than 90 species of birds eat dogwood berries, including catbirds, mockingbirds, robins, thrushes, woodpeckers, vireos, white-throated sparrows, song sparrows, bluebirds, cardinals, and kingbirds. Many warblers and other birds also hunt for insects among dogwood branches and in the furrows of the bark.

CULTURE: Dogwoods grow well in most good garden soils, but prefer well-drained, acid soil that is rich in organic matter. Mulch to keep the soil moist and cool. Partial shade is ideal, although dogwoods will tolerate full sun. Zones 5–9, depending on the species.

- *Ilex* spp. / Hollies

DESCRIPTION: Shrub species of holly are either evergreen or deciduous and bear round, pea-sized berries that are red or black in color. Although birds gobble up the berries of some species as soon as they ripen in fall, others persist on the plants and provide important winter to early spring food. Use these plants, which can range in height from 5 to 30 feet, in foundation plantings, mixed plantings of shrubs and trees, and as specimen plants. Deciduous hollies include possum haw *(Ilex decidua)* and common winterberry (*I. verticillata,* see photo on page 8). Evergreen species include inkberry *(I. glabra),* Meserve hollies *(I. × meserveae),* yaupon *(I. vomitoria),* and Chinese holly *(I. cornuta).* (For information on tree hollies, see "*Ilex* spp." on page 36.)

BIRDS ATTRACTED: Bluebirds, robins, waxwings, catbirds, and mockingbirds are among the species that fancy the berries.

Culture: Deciduous hollies are easy to grow in any good garden soil. They are also easy to transplant. Evergreen hollies grow best in partial shade in acid, loamy soil that is well drained. They are slower-growing and more difficult to establish. Spring planting of balled-and-burlapped or container-grown plants is recommended. Be sure to plant male and female plants of any species you grow to ensure berries; one male will pollinate three female plants. Zones 3 or 4–9, depending on the species.

■ *Rhus* spp. / Sumacs

Description: Sumacs are large shrubs or small trees that produce featherlike compound leaves and cone-shaped clusters of berrylike fruit that are an important source of winter food for birds. They are effective in wild gardens or on banks; since most spread rapidly by suckers, it's best to avoid sites where spreading would be a problem. Staghorn sumac *(Rhus typhina)* is a 10- to 30-foot shrub

*Sumacs (*Rhus *spp.) are best suited to wild gardens. Their conelike fruit clusters are attractive to more than 95 species of birds.*

or small tree and the best garden ornamental. Fragrant sumac *(R. aromatica)* and flameleaf or shining sumac *(R. copallina)* are other species to consider. Lemonade sumac *(R. integrifolia)* is a California native that can be grown in Zones 9 and 10.

BIRDS ATTRACTED: Since sumac fruits persist on the plants into winter, they are an important source of food. More than 95 species of birds have been observed eating them, including towhees, woodpeckers and flickers, chickadees, robins, vireos, thrushes, catbirds, wild turkeys, and bobwhites.

CULTURE: Sumacs will grow in any garden soil in full sun. They can also be planted in difficult sites, including dry sand and rocky hillsides. Zones 3–9, depending on the species.

■ *Rosa* spp. / Roses

DESCRIPTION: Roses are, of course, one of America's most beloved garden flowers, but pampered hybrid teas are not the best roses for a bird garden. To welcome birds, look for shrub roses that bear small hips that they can eat easily. The berries provide important winter food, and the dense branches of these 5- to 15-foot plants provide cover and nest sites as well. Tough, vigorous, disease-resistant plants are also important, because spraying chemical controls will endanger the birds. Shrub roses are effective in perennial and shrub borders, as well as cottage and wild gardens. Multiflora rose *(Rosa multiflora)* bears an abundance of small hips, but is a noxious weed found in many parts of the country because birds have spread the seed far and wide. The large hips of rugosa roses *(R. rugosa)* are showy, but generally too large for birds to eat. Better choices include Carolina or pasture rose *(R. carolina)*, meadow rose *(R. blanda)*, Cherokee rose *(R. laevigata)*, nootka rose *(R. nutkana)*, Virginia rose *(R. virginiana)*, and prairie wild rose *(R. arkansana)*.

BIRDS ATTRACTED: A variety of birds will nest in the thorny branches of large shrub roses, including cardinals, sparrows, towhees, and indigo buntings. These birds, plus thrushes, robins, bluebirds, vireos, quail, and a host of other species, eat the berries, especially in late winter when food is scarce.

CULTURE: Plant roses in full sun with well-drained, rich soil. Zones 3–9, depending on the species.

Brambles (Rubus spp.) such as these black raspberries are as attractive to people as they are to birds.

■ *Rubus* spp. / Brambles

DESCRIPTION: It comes as no surprise that birds eat the fruit of blackberries, raspberries, and other brambles, including tayberries, wineberries, boysenberries, and loganberries. In fact, if you grow any of these crops for your own use, you'll have to fight the birds for them. Brambles also produce dense thickets of thorny canes that provide excellent cover and nesting sites as well. If you protect your bramble crops with netting, plant extras for the birds to enjoy. Brambles are ideal in hedgerows and wild gardens. Ask your local extension service to recommend the best bramble crops for your region.

BIRDS ATTRACTED: Nearly 150 species of birds eat bramble berries, including bluebirds, cardinals, catbirds, grosbeaks, jays, mockingbirds, orioles, phoebes, robins, sparrows, tanagers, vireos, waxwings, and woodpeckers.

CULTURE: Grow brambles in full sun in rich, well-drained soil. Zones 3–10, depending on the species.

Red elderberry (Sambucus racemosa) *produces clusters of yellowish white flowers in late spring followed by showy, round, red berries in late summer.*

■ *Sambucus* spp. / Elderberries

DESCRIPTION: Elderberries bear flat clusters of small white flowers in late spring, followed by large clusters of red or black berrylike fruits. These shrubs or small trees range in height from 6 to as much as 45 feet and have handsome, compound leaves. Elderberries prefer moist soil and are ideal for pond edges, drainage ditches, and other boggy areas. They can also be used in shrub borders and along woodland edges. American elderberry *(Sambucus canadensis)* grows wild throughout the eastern half of the country. Blue elderberry *(S. caerulea)* is a Pacific Coast native. European elder *(S. nigra),* and European red elder *(S. racemosa)* are also suitable.

BIRDS ATTRACTED: Elderberries provide a feast of summer fruit for 120 species of birds or more, including bluebirds, grosbeaks, sparrows, phainopepla, thrashers, catbirds, vireos, finches, doves, woodpeckers, and flickers.

CULTURE: Elderberries are easy to grow in nearly any type of soil, although they grow best in moist sites. If these sprawling plants become overgrown, simply cut them to the ground, and they'll quickly regrow. Zones 4–9.

■ *Vaccinium* spp. / **Blueberries**

DESCRIPTION: Blueberries are another cultivated crop that are every bit as popular with birds as they are with people. They bear urn-shaped flowers in spring, followed by many-seeded berries. The plants range from 8 inches to 18 feet or more. The most common blueberries are lowbush blueberry *(Vaccinium angustifolium)*, highbush blueberry *(V. corymbosum)*, and rabbiteye blueberry *(V. ashei)*. Several other members of the genus produce berries that birds relish, including dryland blueberry *(V. pallidum)*, common deerberry *(V. stamineum)*, and mountain cranberry *(V. vitis idaea)*. Ask your local extension service to recommend blueberries for your area. If you protect blueberry crops with netting or cages, add extra plants for birds. They make ideal additions to foundation plantings, shrub and tree borders, and mixed plantings of shrubs and perennials.

BIRDS ATTRACTED: Bluebirds, robins, orioles, titmice, towhees, jays, thrushes, tanagers, and thrashers are among the many birds that eat blueberries.

CULTURE: Blueberries require acid soil that is moist but well drained. Grow them in full sun for best fruit production, but they will also grow well in partial shade. Zones 2–9, depending on the species.

■ *Viburnum* spp. / **Viburnums**

DESCRIPTION: *Viburnum* is a large genus of showy ornamental shrubs, a few of which can be limbed up to create small trees. They are either deciduous or evergreen, and they range in height from 4 to 30 feet. The clusters of white spring flowers are followed by fleshy, berrylike fruits in red, yellow, blue, or black. On some species, the birds gobble up the fruit soon after they are ripe in late summer or fall; other species, perhaps less palatable, remain on the bushes into winter and early spring, where they provide much-needed food when other sources are scarce. Use viburnums along woodland edges, in shrub and tree borders, and in foundation plantings. Snowball-type viburnums bear round clusters of sterile flowers and do not produce fruit. Red-fruited viburnums include linden vibur-

American cranberry-bush viburnum (Viburnum trilobum) *bears white spring flowers followed by red fruit that matures in midsummer and persists on the plants well into winter.*

num *(V. dilatatum)*, European cranberry-bush viburnum *(Viburnum opulus)*, siebold viburnum *(V. sieboldii)*, American cranberry-bush viburnum *(V. trilobum)*, and Wright viburnum *(V. wrightii)*. Viburnums with blue, blue-black, or black fruit include mapleleaf viburnum *(V. acerifolium)*, withe-rod viburnum *(V. cassinoides)*, arrowwood viburnum *(V. dentatum)*, wayfaring tree *(V. lantana)*, nannyberry viburnum *(V. lentago)*, black haw *(V. prunifolium)*, and Southern black haw *(V. rufidulum)*. Yellow-fruited viburnums are also available, including *V. opulus* 'Xanthocarpum', *V. sargentii* 'Flavum', and *V. dilatatum* 'Xanthocarpum'.

BIRDS ATTRACTED: Robins, grosbeaks, catbirds, thrushes, thrashers, towhees, cardinals, cuckoos, and bluebirds are among the birds that enjoy viburnum berries.

CULTURE: Plant viburnums in full sun and evenly moist, well-drained soil that is slightly acid. Mapleleaf viburnum *(V. acerifolium)* and withe-rod viburnum *(V. cassinoides)* are suitable for shady sites. Zones 3–10, depending on the species.

More Shrubs for Birds

In addition to the shrubs and brambles described in this chapter, the following also are recommended for attracting birds because of the berries or seeds they provide. Plants marked with a symbol (☉) tolerate partial shade.

Arbutus spp. Strawberry tree, madrone. Including *A. unedo* and *A. menziesii.* ☉

Arctostaphylos spp. Manzanitas and bearberries. Including *A. uva-ursi, A. glauca, A. manzanita,* and *A. tomentosa.* ☉

Empetrum spp. Crowberries.

Euonymus alatus. Winged euonymus. ☉

Lindera benzoin. Spicebush. ☉

Mahonia aquifolium. Oregon grape holly. ☉

Myrica spp. Bayberry and waxberries. Including *M. pensylvanica, M. californica,* and *M. cerifera.* ☉

Pyracantha spp. Pyracantha or firethorn. Especially *P. coccinea.* ☉

Rhamnus spp. Buckthorns. Including *R. cathartica, R. alnifolia,* and *A. californica.* ☉

Ribes spp. Gooseberries and currants. ☉

Shepherdia spp. Buffaloberries. Especially *S. canadensis* and *S. argentea.*

Symphoricarpus spp. Snowberries and coralberries. Especially *S. albus, S. occidentalis,* and *S. orbiculatus.* ☉

Taxus spp. Yews. ☉

FLOWERS AND GRASSES FOR A BIRD GARDEN

Trees and shrubs that provide food and cover are by far the most important plants in a garden designed to attract songbirds. However, a flower bed or a meadow garden planted with annuals, perennials, and grasses that produce an abundance of edible seeds is a beneficial addition. Flower seeds attract a variety of seed-eating birds, including cardinals, sparrows, finches, towhees, thrashers, buntings, and juncos. Be sure to include some hummingbird plants, too.

Use the list of annuals, perennials, and grasses on page 54 to get started. All thrive in full sun in average to rich, well-drained soil. Seeds from these plants

Sunflowers are easy to grow and will produce an abundance of seeds for birds. Let birds eat them right in the garden or dry the flowers upside down and save them for winter feeding. You can remove the seeds from the central flower or simply hang the flowers up and let the birds remove them for you.

will provide food from summer into winter. In order to promote seed production, do not deadhead the flowers. Leave the plants standing in the garden after fall frost, and allow birds to feast on the seeds through winter. Cut the plants back in spring.

Plants marked with a butterfly symbol (🦋) also attract butterflies. Plants marked with a hummingbird symbol (🦅) attract hummingbirds.

Annuals & Biennials

Alcea rosea. Garden hollyhock. 🦅

Amaranthus caudatus. Love-lies-bleeding.

Amaranthus hybridus var. *erythrostachys.* Prince's feather.

Briza maxima. Quaking grass.

Calendula officinalis. Pot marigold. 🦋

Callistephus chinensis. China asters.

Centaurea cyanus. Bachelor's button.

Consolida ambigua. Larkspur.

Coreopsis tinctoria. Golden coreopsis. 🦋

Cosmos bipinnatus and *C. sulphureus.* Cosmos.

Dianthus barbatus. Sweet William. 🦋

Eschscholzia californica. California poppy.

Helianthus annuus. Common sunflowers.

Nigella damascena. Love-in-a-mist.

Love-in-a-mist
(*Nigella damascena*)

Papaver spp. Poppies. Especially *P. rhoeas, P. nudicaule,* and *P. somniferum.*

Phlox drummondi. Annual phlox.

Tagetes spp. Marigolds.

Tithonia rotundifolia. Mexican sunflower.

Zinnia spp. Zinnias. Including *Z. officinalis* and *Z. elegans.*

Perennials

Achillea spp. Yarrow.

Aquilegia spp. Columbines.

Asclepias spp. Milkweeds. Including *A. incarnata* (swamp milkweed) and
   A. tuberosa (butterfly weed).

Aster spp. Asters.

Coreopsis lanceolata. Lance-leaved coreopsis.

Coreopsis spp. Coreopsis, tickseed.

Daucus carota. Queen-Anne's-lace.

Echinacea spp. Coneflowers. Including *E. purpurea* (purple coneflower)
   and *E. pallida* (pale coneflower).

Echinops ritro. Globe thistle.

Eupatorium spp. Boneset, Joe-Pye weed.

Fragaria virginiana. Wild strawberry.

Helianthus spp. Perennial sunflowers.

Heliopsis helianthoides. Sunflower heliopsis.

Butterfly weed
(*Asclepias tuberosa*)

Liatris spp. Blazing-stars. 🦋

Papaver orientale. Oriental poppy.

Ratibida pinnata. Gray-headed coneflower.

Rudbeckia spp. Coneflowers, black-eyed Susans. 🦋

Silphium lanciniatum. Compass plant.

Solidago spp. Goldenrods. 🦋

Vernonia noveboracensis. Ironweed. 🦋

Viola spp. Violets. 🦋

Goldenrod 'Golden Fleece' (*Solidago sphacelata* 'Golden Fleece')

Sweet violet *(Viola odorata)*

Vines for Birds

Several species of vines provide berries that birds eat, and their tangled stems create ideal nest sites and cover. Grapes (*Vitis* spp.) are probably the most important vines for feeding birds. They are popular with many species including bluebirds, cardinals, jays, and thrashers. Birds eat cultivated grapes as well as wild species such as summer or pigeon grape *(V. aestivalis)*, winter grape *(V. vulpina)*, fox grape *(V. labrusca)*, riverbank grape *(V. riparia)*, canyon grape *(V. arizonica)*, and California grape *(V. californica)*. Virginia creeper, or woodbine *(Parthenocissus quinquefolia)*, also provides berries for birds as do the greenbriers or catbriers (*Smilax* spp.) and American bittersweet *(Celastris scandens)*. (Beware of Chinese bittersweet, *C. orbiculatus,* which is more rampant and has become a noxious weed in the Northeast.)

Wild grape *(Vitis aestivalis)*

Native grasses are ideal for planting in prairie or meadow gardens, where their seeds will provide food for birds from summer through winter. Use nonnative ornamental grasses as seed sources in flower and shrub borders.

Grasses

Many grasses produce abundant seeds that birds eat. The list below includes just a few native species. Many ornamental grasses that are not native also produce an abundant harvest of seeds. Birds will also appreciate cultivated plots of millet, wheat, or oats. Weedy areas often support foxtails (*Setaria* spp.) and other grasses that birds enjoy.

Andropogon gerardii. Big bluestem.
Andropogon virginicus. Broomsedge bluestem.
Bouteloua curtipendula. Sideoats grama grass.
Buchloe dactyloides. Buffalo grass.
Chasmanthium latifolium. Northern sea oats.
Deschampsia caespitosa. Tufted hairgrass.
Elymus spp. Including *E. canadensis* (Canada wild rye) and
    E. villosus (slender wild rye).
Koeleria cristata. June grass.
Panicum virgatum. Switch grass.
Schizachyrium scoparium. Little bluestem.
Sorgastrum nutans. Indian grass.

CHAPTER 3:

PLANTING FOR HUMMINGBIRDS

Everything about hummingbirds is magical. Nearly every gardener knows that hummingbirds zip from flower to flower to sip nectar. They can miraculously hover in midair, insert their bills deep into a bloom, then back up and probe another flower in the cluster before speeding off. These diminutive, jewellike creatures never cease to amaze. Despite their small size (ruby-throated hummingbirds are only 3 to 3¾ inches long; calliope hummingbirds between 2¾ and 3½ inches), they are spectacular fliers that can make swift, aerial starts and stops like no other bird. Hummingbirds can fly forward at speeds clocked as fast as 50 to 60 miles per hour. In addition to hovering in place, they can also fly straight up, straight down, and backwards.

Western states are rich in both hummingbirds and hummingbird plants. This desert scene features thorny-stemmed ocotillos (Fouquieria spp.), which produce scarlet, orange-red, or creamy yellow flowers that attract hummingbirds as well as orioles. The scarlet, tubular flowers of penstemons or beardtongues (Penstemon spp.) are also ideal hummingbird plants.

Most hummingbirds migrate over long distances. Ruby-throated hummingbirds, the only species that nests east of the Mississippi River, winters from southern Texas to Costa Rica in Central America. In summer, it ranges as far north as southern Canada. Rufus hummingbirds winter in Mexico and summer as far north as southern Alaska and the Yukon Territory. Western species frequently migrate up the Sierra and Rocky mountains, as spring arrives and flowers open.

While gardeners in the eastern states see only ruby-throated hummingbirds, western gardeners routinely see eight or more species. Black-chinned, calliope, broad-tailed, and rufus hummingbirds are widely distributed in the West. (Black-chinned, calliope, ruby-throated, and rufus hummingbirds nest into Canada.) In addition to some of these species, California gardeners also can see Anna's, Costa's, and Allen's hummingbirds. Twenty-one species enter the United States, but most don't penetrate far beyond the Mexican border. Southern Arizona and the Big Bend area in Texas are the best places to see these rarer migrants.

Hummingbird Feeders

Hummingbird feeders offer an ideal way to attract these jewels of the air, and a good way to supplement the flower nectar your garden supplies. Several styles of feeders are available commercially, or you can make your own by putting red nail polish or a red ribbon on the type of water bottle used for pet hamsters and gerbils. Hang your feeder in view of a window so you can enjoy the show.

You can buy packets of nectar mix or make your own using one part ordinary white sugar and four parts water. Boil the mixture and let it cool before filling and hanging the feeder. Store leftover mixture in the refrigerator. It isn't necessary to add red food coloring. Never use honey instead of sugar; it has been shown to support bacterial growth that can be fatal to hummingbirds.

Empty the feeder and change the solution every two to three days (every two days if temperatures are above 60°F) to avoid offering nectar mixture that has been contaminated by bacteria. Always wash out the feeder thoroughly with scalding water before refilling.

Spring-blooming shrubs such as rhododendrons and azaleas attract hungry hummingbirds with their nectar-rich blossoms.

WHAT ATTRACTS HUMMINGBIRDS?

A well-designed bird garden will also attract hummingbirds. Like songbirds, hummingbirds need food, water, cover, and nest sites. Flower nectar provides an important part of every hummingbird's diet. Tubular or trumpet-shaped blooms that are bright red or orange in color attract them like magnets. Although a hummingbird's slender, pointed bill is designed specifically for feeding from tubular flowers, they also visit many other kinds of flowers, from white and lilac hosta flowers to zinnias, begonias, and sweet William. Hummingbirds have such fast metabolism that they must feed almost constantly during daylight hours. (A hummingbird's tongue has either a tubular or brushlike tip; to sip nectar, it opens its beak slightly and laps the nectar with the tip of the tongue.) They store food in their crops to sustain them overnight. In cool weather or during cold spring nights, they can temporarily enter a state of dormancy, called torpor, to conserve food reserves. Torpid birds have lowered body temperatures, heart rates, and breathing rates.

Use the lists in this chapter to identify plants that will attract hummingbirds to your garden. Plan for a constant supply of blooms from late spring or early summer to late summer or early fall, depending on when hummingbirds are in your area. (Wild bird centers or birding clubs can tell you when they should be in your area; gardeners in the warmest parts of the Southwest can have hummingbirds year-round.) You can add annuals and perennials that attract them into any of your beds and borders, or plant a garden that features only hummingbird flowers. Add shrubs and vines that attract hummingbirds to shrub borders and foundation plantings. Vines are especially effective when trained on a trellis near a window so you can watch the birds feeding, but a freestanding arbor or a trellis behind flower beds is also effective. Vines can also be trained up fences and trees and allowed to spill over shrubs.

Hummingbirds guard feeding and nesting territories during the breeding season, so try to scatter plants that attract them throughout your yard. (Males guard feeding territories and use them to attract females. The females, which build the nests and raise the young alone, establish nesting territories and drive away other hummingbirds.) Or plant two hummingbird gardens, one in the backyard and another in the front, out of sight of the first.

In addition to nectar, some species also eat flower pollen and tree sap. Hummingbirds have been observed feeding on sap running from tree wounds, as well as from the holes drilled by sapsuckers.

Insects are an important part of every hummingbird's diet. They eat a wide variety of them, including aphids, gnats, mosquitoes, flying ants, leafhoppers, and flies, as well as small beetles, bugs, and weevils. Beneficial spiders and parasitic wasps are also common fare. Hummingbirds frequently catch insects and spiders on the flowers they frequent in their search for nectar. Daddy longlegs, or harvestmen, are another common prey. Ruby-throated hummingbirds have been observed picking insects out of spider webs.

TIPS FOR SUCCESS

Orioles feed on many plants that attract hummingbirds, including trumpet vines (Campsis radicans), honeysuckle (Lonicera spp.), and daylilies. They also visit hummingbird feeders for nectar. Special oriole feeders are available, which are orange in color and somewhat larger than hummingbird feeders. Orioles prefer a slightly more diluted sugar mixture. Boil one part sugar in six parts water. Replace the mixture and clean the feeder every two to three days, just as you would for hummingbirds.

Bee balm (Monarda didyma) *is a member of the mint family with fragrant leaves and clusters of red flowers. It spreads quickly by underground runners, so grow it in wild areas or plant it in bottomless buckets sunk in the soil to contain its spreading.*

Other Hummingbird Garden Features. A yard that offers a mix of sun and shade is ideal for attracting hummingbirds. Many of the flowers they feed from grow best in sunny beds, borders, or meadow plantings. Wooded areas provide ideal nest sites. Hummingbirds construct their tiny, cup-shaped nests from a variety of materials that are fastened together with spider webs. (An organic garden that is rich in spiders will ensure a ready supply for your visitors.) The sites selected vary by species, but areas of open or dense woods or forest margins, sometimes over a stream, are common. They construct nests from such materials as milkweed or thistledown, soft ferns, moss, and grasses. Several species decorate the outside of the nest with lichen until it blends in with the branch to which it is attached.

Hummingbirds build their diminutive nests from a variety of materials, such as milkweed or thistle down, held together by spider webs. The outsides of the nests are often decorated with bits of lichen and moss.

Blazing stars or gayfeathers (Liatris spp.) are native wildflowers in the daisy family. They attract visitors such as this ruby-throated hummingbird as well as butterflies.

To make a birdbath or other water feature especially appealing to hummingbirds, consider adding a device that produces a fine spray or mist above it. (These are available from wild bird centers.) Hummingbirds are designed for a life in the air and will actually bathe by repeatedly flying through the mist. They will also alight on a twig positioned near water.

FLOWERS FOR HUMMINGBIRDS

Because many annuals bloom from spring or early summer through frost, they provide a steady supply of nectar for hummingbirds all season long. Mix these reliable, easy-to-grow plants into beds and borders along with perennials to create a showy display that both you and the hummingbirds will adore. Or grow a bed of annuals alone that changes design every year. You can also edge shrub borders or foundation plantings with annuals, or plant them in the herb or vegetable garden. Gardeners in southern zones — in the South, Southwest, and lower elevations of California — will find a number of tender perennials that are grown as annuals in the North but can be grown as perennials in the South.

■ *Alcea rosea* / Hollyhocks

DESCRIPTION: The tall spikes of hollyhocks appeal to hummingbirds and gardeners alike. Look for single-flowered types, which have showy summer blooms in burgundy, red, deep pink, orange-yellow, and white. Although they are officially biennials, hollyhocks are short-lived perennials in the right conditions. They also reseed.

CULTURE: Plant hollyhocks in deep, rich, well-drained soil in full sun. A site out of the wind is important; otherwise these tall plants need staking. Sow seed indoors in winter for bloom the following summer, or sow outdoors in summer for bloom the following summer. Zones 2–9.

■ *Antirrhinum majus* / Snapdragons

DESCRIPTION: Snapdragons are perennials grown as half-hardy annuals. These erect or spreading plants bear spikes of red, burgundy, orange, pink, yellow, and white blooms. Their early spring blooms provide nectar when hummingbird flowers can be scarce. Plants range from dwarfs under 1 foot to 3-foot plants that require staking.

CULTURE: Snapdragons prefer cool temperatures and will even survive light frost. Plant them outdoors in full sun and rich, well-drained soil as soon as the soil can be worked in spring. Remove spent blooms to prolong flowering. Sow seeds outdoors in a shaded spot in late summer for a fall crop of blooms.

Snapdragons (Antirrhinum majus) *are easy-to-grow annuals with spikes of brightly colored blooms that attract hummingbirds.*

■ *Aquilegia* spp. / Columbines

DESCRIPTION: Columbines provide an important source of nectar for hummingbirds in spring and early summer. The blue-green compound foliage is delicate-looking and attractive. Wild columbine *(A. canadensis)* bears dangling red-and-yellow flowers on 1- to 3-foot plants; crimson columbine *(A. formosa)* resembles it, but is native to the western United States. Hybrid columbines with red and pink flowers are also good choices.

CULTURE: Grow columbines in full sun to partial shade. Moist, well-drained, sandy to loamy soil is ideal. Zones 4–9.

■ *Canna* × *generalis* / Cannas

DESCRIPTION: Cannas are tuberous-rooted tender perennials that are grown as annuals in northern zones. They feature bold, tropical-looking leaves and clusters of showy red, orange, or yellow summer flowers. Height can range from 3 to 6 feet or more. Cannas generally look best planted in a bed by themselves or among tall, bold perennials, large annuals, and ornamental grasses.

CULTURE: Rich, well-drained, evenly moist soil and a site in full sun is essential. Plant outdoors in spring when soil temperatures reach 65°F — about the time tomatoes can be planted. Roots can be dug in fall and overwintered indoors like dahlias. Grow cannas as perennials in Zone 8 and south.

■ *Digitalis* spp. / Foxgloves

DESCRIPTION: Foxgloves bear erect spikes of tubular flowers in deep pink, rose, white, or yellow atop rosettes of large, broad, lance-shaped leaves. Common foxglove *(Digitalis purpurea)* is a biennial or short-lived perennial that ranges from 2 to 5 feet. Strawberry foxglove *(D. × mertonensis)* bears rose pink flowers and is a short-lived perennial. It is 3 to 4 feet tall.

CULTURE: Grow foxgloves in full sun or partial shade in evenly moist, well-drained soil that is rich in organic matter. Both species will self-sow. Divide *D. × mertonensis* every two to three years to maintain its perennial character. Zones 3–8, depending on the species.

Foxglove (Digitalis purpurea) *produces spikes of trumpet-shaped, rosy-purple, pink, or white flowers in spring and early summer.*

Hummingbirds will visit daylilies with yellow or orange flowers, but they are particularly attracted to red-hued cultivars including 'Pardon Me', 'Christmas Carol', 'Royal Mountie', and 'Scarlet Apache'.

■ *Hemerocallis* spp. / **Daylilies**

DESCRIPTION: Daylilies produce trumpet-shaped flowers, each of which lasts only a day, above clumps of strap-shaped leaves in summer. Plants range from 2 to over 4 feet in height. Hummingbirds visit lemon daylily *(H. lilio-asphodelus)* and tawny daylily *(H. fulva)* as well as hybrids with vivid red, orange, pink, and yellow flowers.

CULTURE: Grow daylilies in full sun in average to rich soil that is moist but well drained. They will also tolerate light shade. Zones 2–9, depending on the species.

Common rose mallow (Hibiscus moscheutos) *is a hardy perennial that bears its dramatic pink, red, or white flowers all summer long.*

■ *Hibiscus* spp. / Hibiscus, rose mallow

DESCRIPTION: These tropical-looking plants bear large red, rose, pink, or white, saucer-shaped flowers atop 5- to 8-foot plants. The leaves are broad and maplelike. Both scarlet rose mallow *(Hibiscus coccineus)* and rose mallow *(H. moscheutos)* are good choices.

CULTURE: Grow hibiscus in moist, well-drained soil that is rich in organic matter. They will grow in full sun or partial shade. Zones 5–10, depending on the species.

- *Lilium* spp. / Lilies

DESCRIPTION: The trumpet-, cup-, or bowl-shaped flowers of many lilies are ideal for attracting hummingbirds. These stately bulbs range from 2 to 8 feet or more in height and have narrow grasslike or lance-shaped leaves. Hummingbirds visit several native species of lilies that have red to orange-red or orange flowers, including Canada lily *(Lilium canadense)*, wood lily *(L. philadelphicum)*, Turk's-cap lily *(L. superbum)*, and tiger lily *(L. lancifolium)*. Hummingbirds would also appreciate the many hybrid lilies with bright flowers that are available.

CULTURE: Lilies demand well-drained soil that is deep, rich, and loamy. The pH should be neutral to slightly acid, although some species tolerate alkaline soils. A site in full sun is best, but native lilies will tolerate partial shade. Zones 3–9, depending on the species.

- *Lobelia cardinalis* / Cardinal flower

DESCRIPTION: No hummingbird garden should be without a clump of this native wildflower, which bears spikes of scarlet flowers in late summer above clumps of lance-shaped leaves. Plants reach 2 to 4 feet. Cultivars with burgundy and ruby-red flowers are available. (See photo on page 6.)

CULTURE: Cardinal flowers need constantly moist soil in partial to full shade. Plant them along streams or ponds, and even drainage ditches. Divide plants every two years; they can be short-lived, and division helps keep them vigorous. Zones 2–9

- *Monarda didyma* / Bee balm, bergamot, Oswego tea

DESCRIPTION: As its common name implies, bee balm is attractive to bees, but hummingbirds and butterflies also frequent its somewhat ragged-looking clusters of tube-shaped flowers. The leaves are fragrant and minty and the plants range from 2 to 4 feet. 'Marshall's Delight' is a pink-flowered, mildew-resistant cultivar. 'Gardenview Scarlet' bears large red flowers and is also mildew-resistant. (See photo on page 65.)

CULTURE: Grow bee balm in any good soil that remains evenly moist. The plants will grow in full sun or partial shade. Since they spread quickly, divide

Asiatic hybrid lilies, such as this 'Red Night', bloom early in lily season, are easy to grow, and multiply quickly.

them frequently in spring. Or plant them in an out-of-the-way spot in a wild garden where they can spread unimpeded. Zones 4–8.

■ *Nicotiana* spp. / Flowering tobacco

DESCRIPTION: Hummingbirds visit the fragrant trumpets of flowering tobaccos, which are tender perennials grown as annuals. *Nicotiana* × *sanderae* and its cultivars, including 'Crimson Rock', 'Breakthrough Mix', and 'Niki Series', are especially effective because they come in crimson red, rose pink, or white. *N. alata* and *N. sylvestris* also are effective; plants with white flowers are most common, but cultivars with red, pink, or purplish blooms are available. Plants range from 1 to 3 feet.

CULTURE: Plant flowering tobacco in partial shade or full sun. Grow from seed sown in the garden after all danger of frost has past. Or start seedlings indoors six to eight weeks before the last spring frost and move transplants to the garden two weeks after the last frost date. Do not cover the seed, as it requires light to germinate.

■ *Penstemon* spp. / Penstemons, beardtongues

DESCRIPTION: These spring- and summer-blooming perennials bear racemes of two-lipped tubular flowers in bright colors, including scarlet, purple, lavender-blue, yellow, or white, on plants that range from 3 or 4 inches to 6 feet or more. Most penstemons are native to western North America and can be difficult to grow outside their native habitats. Hybrid penstemons are among the best choices for eastern gardens, where summer heat and humidity are problematic. These include 'Firebird', 'Ruby', and 'Garnet', along with hairy beardtongue *(Penstemon hirsutus)*. Other penstemons to try include common beardtongue *(P. barbatus)* and its cultivar 'Prairie Fire', *P. pinifolius,* and *P. smallii.*

CULTURE: Penstemons require well-drained sandy or loamy soil that is rich in humus. Grow them in full sun or light shade. Divide plants every four to five years to keep them vigorous. Zones 3–8.

Hummingbirds will visit flowers such as these petunias. Planting them in window boxes will give you a front-row seat for easy viewing. Also consider planting tubs and containers on decks and patios with hummingbird-attracting plants.

■ *Petunia* × *hybrida* / **Petunias**

DESCRIPTION: Petunias are sprawling, 8- to 18-inch plants that bear trumpet-shaped blooms in red, deep pink, purple, blue, and white. Many striped or barred types are available, too, including red and pink blooms with stripes or white edges. For hummingbirds, avoid double flowers. Chose multiflora or milliflora types, which have smaller and more plentiful flowers and are more disease-resistant than grandifloras.

CULTURE: Move transplants to the garden after danger of frost has passed. They prefer full sun, warm weather, and good, well-drained garden soil. Water frequently during hot weather. Shear plants back and feed them after the main flush of blooms to encourage them to produce additional flowers.

Early-blooming flowers such as this creeping phlox (Phlox subulata) *provide an important source of nectar for hummingbirds in spring.*

▪ *Phlox* spp. / Phlox

DESCRIPTION: Phlox bear tubular flowers with five petals and can range from ground-hugging 4-inch plants to stately 4-foot plants for the perennial border. The flowers can be lavender, purple, pink, red, or white. Hummingbirds will visit a variety of phlox species, regardless of their color, including wild blue phlox *(P. divaricata)*, Douglas's phlox *(P. douglasii)*, creeping phlox *(P. stolonifera)*, Carolina phlox *(P. carolina)*, moss pink *(Phlox subulata)*, garden phlox *(P. paniculata)*, and wild sweet William *(P. maculata)*. Red-flowered selections hummingbirds especially enjoy include *P. paniculata* 'Starfire', *P. douglasii* 'Cracker Jack', and *P. subulata* 'Scarlet Flame'.

CULTURE: Grow woodland natives *P. divaricata* and *P. stolonifera* in partial to full shade in rich, evenly moist soil. Grow the other species in full sun or very light shade. *P. douglasii* and *P. subulata* will grow in sandy or loamy soil that is well drained. The others require rich soil that is evenly moist but well drained. Zones 2–9, depending on the species.

■ *Salvia* spp. / Sages

DESCRIPTION: Hummingbirds visit several scarlet-flowered members of this genus. Scarlet sage *(Salvia splendens),* probably the most common, bears erect spikes of flaming red flowers on 1- to 3-foot plants. Texas sage *(S. coccinea)* bears its red blooms on 1- to 2-foot plants. Both are tender perennials grown as annuals in the North. Pineapple sage *(S. elegans)* flowers in the fall on 3- to 4-foot plants and is a perennial in Zone 9 and south. Autumn sage *(S. gregii)* is a Texas native with red to purplish red flowers that is hardy in Zone 7 and south. Both are grown as annuals in the North.

Scarlet sage (Salvia splendens) *bears its flowers all summer long. Edging a bed with a block of these flaming red blooms or mixing them in with annuals or perennials is a sure-fire way to roll out the welcome mat for hummingbirds.*

More Flowers for Hummingbirds

Once blazing red flowers lure hummingbirds to your garden, they're likely to sip from a variety of blooms. Here are some more flowers you can add to your plantings.

Annuals

Begonia × Semperflorens-cultorum hybrids. Wax begonias.

Cleome hasslerana. Spider flower, cleome.

Consolida spp. Larkspur.

Dahlia hybrids. Dahlias.

Dianthus barbatus. Sweet William.

Gladiolus spp. Gladiolus. Including *G. communis,* hardy in Zones 6–10, and *G. × hortulanus,* hardy in Zones 7–10, but grown as an annual in the North.

Miriabilis jalapa. Four-o'clocks, marvel-of-Peru.

Pelargonium spp. Zonal geraniums.

Scabiosa atropurpurea. Pincushion flower.

Tagetes spp. Marigolds.

Tithonia rotundifolia. Mexican sunflower.

Zinnia spp. Zinnias.

Spider flower *(Cleome hasslerana)*

Perennials

Buddleia spp. Butterfly bushes.

Castileja spp. Paintbrushes.

Crocosmia spp. Montbretia, crocosmia.
Including *C. masoniorum* and its cultivar
'Firebird', *C.* × *crocosmiiflora* 'Emily
McKenzie', and hybrids such as 'Lucifer'
and 'Emberglow'.

Delphinium spp. Delphiniums.
Especially *D. cardinale* and *D. nudicale*

Dianthus spp. Pinks, carnations.
Including *D.* × *Allwoodii, D. deltoides,* and
D. plumarius.

Epilobium angustifolium. Fireweed.

Gentiana septemfida var. *lagodechiana.*
Crested gentian.

Heuchera sanguinea. Coralbells

Hosta spp. Hostas, funkia, plantain lilies.

Kniphofia uvuaria. Red-hot poker.

Liatris spp. Gayfeathers, blazing-stars.

Lycoris spp. Spider lilies, magic lilies.
Especially *L. radiata* and *L. squamigera.*

Saponaria officinalis. Bouncing bet.

Scabiosa caucasica. Pincushion flower.

Silene spp. Catchfly, campion.
Including *S. virginica* and *S. regia.*

Yucca spp. Yucca, Adam's-needle.

Coral bells *(Heuchera sanguinea)*

CULTURE: Plant salvias outdoors in full sun after all danger of frost has passed. Give plenty of water in dry weather. In the South, Southwest, and lower elevations of California, plants benefit from light to moderate shade. Take cuttings of perennial salvias in fall and root and overwinter them indoors.

■ *Tropaeolum majus* / Garden nasturtium

DESCRIPTION: Nasturtiums are annuals that bear round leaves and showy red, orange, or yellow trumpetlike flowers all summer long. Both low-growing and climbing plants are available. Climbing nasturtiums require a trellis and can reach 10 feet in height. In addition to visiting the flowers for nectar, hummingbirds also undoubtedly feast on the aphids that commonly attack nasturtiums.

CULTURE: Grow nasturtiums in average to poor, well-drained soil; rich soil encourages lush foliage at the expense of flowers. Sow seed outside two weeks before the last spring frost. Nasturtiums transplant with difficulty but can be grown indoors in peat pots and moved after the last spring frost. These plants prefer cool temperatures and will not grow well in the Southeast during the hot summer months.

■ *Verbena* spp. / Garden verbena

DESCRIPTION: Verbenas bear rounded clusters of small fragrant flowers in red, pink, purple, yellow, and white from summer to fall. The plants can be trailing or upright, but are generally under 1 foot in height. Common garden verbena *(Verbena × hybrida),* a tender perennial grown as an annual, comes in a variety of colors, including vivid scarlet. *V. peruviana* bears red flowers and is hardy in Zone 9 and south, but is commonly grown as an annual in the North. *V.* 'Taylortown Red' and *V.* 'Flame' have vivid scarlet flowers and are hardy in Zones 6–9.

CULTURE: Grow verbenas in full sun, except in the Deep South and desert areas, where light shade is best to reduce drought stress. Transplant after all danger of frost has past. Deadhead flowers to keep new blooms coming. In areas where they cannot be grown as perennials, take cuttings in fall and root and overwinter them indoors.

Trumpet vine (Campsis radicans) *is a vigorous climber that produces its red-orange trumpets in summer and early fall.*

VINES FOR HUMMINGBIRDS

Vines are stunning trained over a trellis near a patio or on a deck, or at the back of a flower garden. They also have a nice effect covering a fence.

■ *Campsis* / **Trumpet vine**

DESCRIPTION: The orange to orange-red blooms of trumpet vine are classic hummingbird plants. *Campsis radicans* bears an abundance of orange, orange-red, or yellow 3-inch-long trumpets in summer and early fall. 'Crimson Trumpet' has red flowers without orange overtones. *C.* × *tagliabuana* 'Mme. Galen' bears rich orange-pink trumpets. Both are woody vines that climb to between 30 and 40 feet and bear compound leaves.

CULTURE: Trumpet vines are easy to grow in any soil and can be rampant in rich soil. Full sun is best, but plants will tolerate light shade. Prune the plants in spring to keep them in bounds and to keep them from becoming top-heavy. Top-heavy plants can pull away from their support. Zones 5–9.

■ *Ipomoea* / Ipomoeas, morning glories

DESCRIPTION: Hummingbirds adore several of the easy-to-grow annual vines in this genus, which bear their blooms from early summer to fall. Cardinal climber *(Ipomoea multifida)* bears crimson trumpets with white eyes and has triangular-oval leaves. Cypress vine *(I. quamoclit)* also bears red trumpet-shaped flowers but has fernlike leaves. Red morning glory *(I. coccinea)* has fragrant red flowers and heart-shaped leaves. All generally climb to between 10 and 12 feet in an average summer; they can reach 25 feet or more in southern climates, where the growing season is long.

CULTURE: Grow ipomoeas in well-drained, average soil in a warm, sunny location, and keep the plants well watered. For best results, nick the hard seed coats with a nail file, or soak them for eight hours in tepid water before sowing. Although the seeds can be sown outdoors after all danger of frost has passed, it's best to start them indoors six to eight weeks before the last frost. Sow seeds in peat pots, and transplant the seedlings with care, as they resent being disturbed.

■ *Lonicera* spp. / Honeysuckle

DESCRIPTION: Both scarlet trumpet honeysuckle *(Lonicera* × *brownii)* and trumpet honeysuckle *(L. sempervirens)* make good additions to a hummingbird garden. Both bear clusters of narrow, red-to-orange trumpets in spring or early summer on twining, woody stems with oval leaves. Plants range from 12 to 20 feet in height. *L.* × *brownii* 'Dropmore Scarlet' has vivid red flowers that appear from early summer to fall.

CULTURE: Grow honeysuckles in moist, well-drained soil that is slightly acid to

Trumpet honeysuckle (Lonicera sempervirens) *is an easy-to-grow vine that bears clusters of narrow, trumpet-shaped blooms in spring.*

Common lilacs (Syringa vulgaris) *bear spring clusters of fragrant flowers in pale lilac, deep purple, pink, magenta, or white.*

near neutral. A site in full sun is best, but plants will tolerate light shade. Prune plants immediately after they flower to control the shape; be sure not to prune in late winter to early spring or you will remove most of the flower buds. Zones 4–9.

- ### *Phaseolus coccineus* / Scarlet runner beans

DESCRIPTION: Scarlet runner beans are tender perennials commonly grown as annuals in vegetable gardens rather than flower beds. Hummingbirds don't care where they find the racemes of scarlet flowers. Plants have attractive, blue-green leaves and will climb to 10 feet. The flowers are followed by tasty beans with somewhat fuzzy pods.

CULTURE: Grow scarlet runner beans in rich, well-drained soil in full sun. Sow seeds outdoors after the last spring frost date.

TREES AND SHRUBS FOR HUMMINGBIRDS

Hummingbirds visit the flowers of many kinds of trees and shrubs. Consider including one or more of the following in your butterfly garden. Plants marked with a bird symbol ( ) will also attract songbirds.

Abelia grandiflora. Glossy abelia.
Aesculus pavia. Red buckeye.
Albizia julibrissin. Mimosa, silk tree.
Caragana arborescens. Siberian pea-tree.
Chaenomeles speciosa. Common flowering quince.
Crataegus phaenopyrum. Washington hawthorn.
Hibiscus syriacus. Rose-of-Sharon, shrub althaea.
Kolkwitzia amabilis. Beautybush.
Malus spp. Crabapples, apples.
Rhododendron spp. Rhododendrons and azaleas.
Robinia pseudoacacia. Black locust.
Syringa spp. Lilacs.
Vitex agnus-castus. Chaste tree.
Weigela florida. Old-fashioned weigela.

HUMMINGBIRD PLANTS FOR SOUTHERN ZONES

A wealth of hummingbird plants exist for gardeners living in Zones 8, 9, 10, and 11. The following list includes some of the best plants to consider, but it is by no means complete. Many of the plants below come in a wide range of colors: when planting any hummingbird garden, take time to search out the brightest-colored cultivars you can find.

Many of these plants can be grown as pot plants that can summer outdoors and spend winter protected in a greenhouse or indoors. These include *Abutilon, Aloe, Fuchsia, Hibiscus,* and *Justicia.* In some cases, all they need to survive outdoors a zone north of where they are hardy is winter protection for a few crucial months when temperatures dip too low.

Abutilon spp. Flowering maple. Zones 9–11.

Agave spp. Century plant. Especially *A. americana.* Zones 9–11.

Aloe spp. Aloes. Including *Aloe arborescens, A. aristata, A. brevifolia, A. ferox, A. humilis, A. saponaria,* and *A. striata.* Zones 9–11.

Caesalpinia gilliesii. Bird-of-paradise shrub. Zones 8–11.

Callistemon spp. Bottlebrushes. Including *C. citrinus, C. rigidus,* and *C. eriophylla.* Zones 8–11.

Cercidium floridum. Palo verde. Zones 9–11.

Cestrum spp. Cestrums or jessamines. Including *C. aurantiacum, C. elegans,* and *C. fasciculatum.* Zones 9–11.

Chilopsis spp. Desert willow. Including *Chilopsis linearis.* Zones 8–11.

Citrus spp. Citrus trees, including orange, lemon, grapefruit trees. Zones 9–11.

Costus spp. Spiral gingers. Including *C. pulverulentus* and *C. speciosus.* Zones 9–11.

Cuphea spp. Cigar plant or firecracker plant. Including *C. ignea* and *C. micropetala.* Zones 9–11.

Delonix regia. Flame tree or royal poinciana. Zones 9–11.

Erythrina cristi-galli. Cockspur coral tree. Zones 9–11.

Erythrina spp. Coral trees. Including *E. crista-galli* and *E.* × *bidwillii.* Zones 8–11.

Eucalyptus spp. Eucalyptus or gum tree. Zones 9–11.

Fountain bush (Russelia equisetiformis)

Fuchsia 'Swingtime'

Feijoa sellowiana. Pineapple guava. Zones 8–11.

Fouquieria splendens. Ocotillo. Zones 8–11.

Fuchsia spp. Fuchsias. Zones 9–11.

Hamelia patens. Scarlet bush. Zones 9–11.

Hedychium spp. Ginger lilies. Including *H. aurantiacum* and *H. coccineum.*
    Zones 8–11.

Heliconia spp. False bird-of-paradise.
    Including *H. brasiliensis, H. latispatha,* and *H. schiedeana.* Zones 9–11.

Hesperaloe parviflora. Red yucca. Zones 6–10.

Hibiscus rosa-sinensis. Hibiscus. Zones 9–11.

Ipomosis aggregata. Scarlet gilia. Zones 7–11.

Justicia spp. Shrimp plant, Chuparosa. Including *J. brandegeana* and *J. californica.* Zones 8–11.

Lantana spp. Lantana, shrub verbena. Including *L. camara* and *L. montevidensis.* Zones 9–11.

Melaleuca spp. Bottlebrushes. Zones 10–11.

Nerium oleander. Common oleander. Zones 8–11.

Nicotiana glauca. Tree tobacco. Zones 9–11.

Pentas lanceolata. Egyptian star-cluster. Zones 9–11.

Quisqualis indica. Rangoon creeper. Zones 9–11.

Ruellia graecizans. Red ruellia. Zones 9–11.

Russelia equisetiformis. Fountain bush. Zones 8–11.

Sesbaina spp. Scarlet wisteria tree. Including *S. grandiflora, S. punicea,* and *S. tripetii.* Zones 8–11.

Yucca elata. Soaptree yucca. Zones 8–11.

Zauschneria californica. California fuchsia. Zones 8–11.

Vines

Antigonon leptopus. Coral vine. Zones 8–10.

Bignonia capreolata. Cross vine or trumpet flower. Zones 6–10.

Disticitis buccinatoira. Blood-red trumpet vine. Zones 10–11.

Pyrostegia venusta. Flame vine. Zones 10–11.

Tecomaria capensis. Cape honeysuckle. Zones 10–11.

Tropaeolum speciosum. Vermillion nasturtium. Zones 7–9.

Chapter 4:

Attracting Butterflies

Butterflies bring a whole new dimension to a garden. Not only do they add color that flutters and dances over your beds and borders, but watching and learning about them can become a fascinating lifelong hobby. The plants that attract butterflies are easy to incorporate in any garden, because they include so many beloved annuals, perennials, and herbs. Asters, marigolds, sunflowers, and zinnias are just some of the common flowers that butterflies visit.

To plan and plant a butterfly garden, it helps to know a bit about their life cycles. Attracting adult butterflies is the objective of everyone who plants a butterfly garden, but simply dotting a few well-known butterfly flowers around your yard won't necessarily lead to success. You'll have better luck if you take their entire cycle into consideration.

Sweet William (Dianthus barbatus) *bears clusters of fragrant flowers in pinks, reds, and whites that attract a variety of butterflies, such as this red-spotted purple.*

Several species of swallowtails lay their eggs on members of the parsley family. This is an anise swallowtail caterpillar feeding on fennel.

Reproduction is the main goal of all adult butterflies. In fact, some adult butterflies do not feed at all; they simply mate, lay eggs, and die. (You can attract even these species by growing the plants they lay eggs on.) Many, of course, visit flowers to sip nectar in the course of finding a mate and laying eggs. Others feed on sap running from tree wounds, rotting fruit, or even scat (animal droppings) and carrion.

Successful butterfly gardens include plants for butterfly larvae, or caterpillars, as well as nectar for adults, and that's where things can get a little complicated. Some species require a specific type of plant for their larvae. Monarch butterflies will lay eggs only on milkweeds (*Asclepias* spp.), for example. Pipevine swallowtails need pipevines, or Dutchman's pipes (*Aristolochia* spp.). Zebra swallowtails lay only on pawpaws (*Asimina* spp.) and related plants. Gulf fritillaries prefer pas-

Joe-Pye weed (Eupatorium fistulosum) *attracts an abundance of swallowtails and other butterflies when it flowers in the fall.*

sionflowers (*Passiflora* spp.) Other species are less particular. The American painted lady lays eggs on a wide variety of plants in the daisy family, Compostiae. Viceroys lay on willows, poplars, and a range of fruit trees. Western tiger swallowtails lay on sycamores, willows, poplars, and aspens. The best approach is to include an assortment of plants for larvae; if you have a specific species you would like to attract, plant host plants for that species. Field guides are a good source of information on host plants for each species.

Once the eggs hatch, the larvae, or caterpillars, become world-class eating machines. They consume plant leaves and stems at an enormous rate and grow at amazing speeds. (At this stage, butterfly gardening can seem at odds with the goals of a conventional garden, especially when the caterpillars are chomping on cabbages or parsley.) The caterpillars molt several times as they grow, eventually molting a final time to form a chrysalis. It is during the chrysalis stage that nearly all of the caterpillar's tissues are broken down and transformed. The end result, when the chrysalis opens, is a butterfly. Newly emerged butterflies have fat bodies and wrinkled wings; they have to pump the fluid from their bodies into their wings, causing the wings to expand. Once the wings have dried and stiffened, the new butterfly is ready to fly.

Several generations of butterflies are born each season. At the end of the summer, butterflies have a variety of strategies for overwintering. Some overwinter as eggs and chrysalises — often in leaf litter or attached to host plants. There are also species that roll themselves in leaves and overwinter as caterpillars; others hibernate as adults in buildings and tree hollows. Some simply die off in the North and repopulate their northern ranges from southern populations that gradually move northward during the course of the summer. Monarchs migrate south each fall, to overwinter in central Mexico and southern California. Other species, including painted ladies and buckeyes, also migrate on a limited basis.

BUTTERFLY GARDEN FEATURES

Start your butterfly garden in a sunny spot that is protected from prevailing winds. A barrier planting of trees and shrubs is ideal; butterflies will appreciate a relatively windless spot where they can fly without being buffeted about. Trellised vines, and even tall annuals or perennials, can also help cut down on wind. In addition to planting butterfly-attracting plants in beds and borders, use them along woodland edges, meadow plantings, and in front of foundation shrubs.

Be sure to include both flowers for nectar and plants for larvae. Try to plant flowers that will bloom in spring, summer, and fall to provide nectar sources all season. Perennials will produce a wide variety of flowers and a progression of blooms. Adding long-blooming annuals will help ensure a steady supply of nectar all summer long.

TIPS FOR SUCCESS

Leaving a weedy patch or two in your yard can be an ideal strategy for increasing butterfly populations. The larvae of painted ladies feed on burdock (*Arctium lappa*). Several species, including buckeyes and variegated fritillary, visit plantains to lay eggs. Nettles (*Urtica* spp.) host the larvae of Milbert's tortoiseshell, question marks, and red admirals. Common milkweed (*Asclepias syriaca*), thistles (*Cirsium* spp.), dock (*Rumex* spp.), Queen-Anne's-lace (*Daucus carota*), and beggar-ticks (*Bidens* spp.) are other suitable plants for a weedy butterfly nursery.

Many species of skippers are attracted to grasses, including bluegrass, Bermuda grass (*Cynodon dactylon*), panic grass (*Panicum* spp.), and sedges (*Carex* spp.), which can be allowed to grow in a weedy area.

Single-flowered hollyhocks and daisy flowers such as these yellow marguerites are both attractive to a wide variety of nectar-seeking butterflies.

Here are some other features you can include to make "your" butterflies feel at home.

Sunning Spots. Butterflies will use areas covered with low ground covers, grasses, or clovers to sun themselves. Since they are cold-blooded, sunning helps them regulate their temperatures. Providing a flat rock in a sunny, windless spot along the edge of your butterfly garden is also a good idea.

Water. There are several ways to provide butterflies with water. A conventional birdbath or other shallow container that is filled with flat stones can provide a safe drinking spot. The stones should emerge from the water, allowing butterflies to alight and drink without getting wet. A low spot that remains moist, or that you keep moist by regular watering, also provides a suitable drinking spot. Butterflies will also visit muddy or sandy spots along streams and pools.

Varying Environments. The more types of habitats your yard provides, the more species of butterflies you are likely to attract. Boggy areas, shady wooded areas, woodland edges, sunny meadows, and conventional beds and borders will all attract butterflies.

A tiger swallowtail probes in mud for salt and other nutrients.

Lance-leaved coreopsis (Coreopsis lanceolata) *produces a bounty of butterfly-attracting flowers from late spring through summer.*

*Eastern tailed blue butterfly
(shown actual size)*

FLOWERS FOR BUTTERFLIES

Butterflies visit literally thousands of different plants, both to sip nectar and to lay their eggs. A few plant families are especially important to them, however, either as nectar sources, larval plants, or both. If you include some plants from each of the families described next, you will increase your chances of attracting a variety of butterflies. See "More Flowers for Butterflies" on page 106 for a list of additional butterfly plants that do not belong to the plant families listed next.

Even the common oxeye daisy will provide food for welcome visitors.

Purple coneflower (Echinacea purpurea) *is a tough, easy-to-grow wildflower that thrives in sun and blooms all summer.*

Daisies. Many kinds of butterflies visit members of the daisy family, Compositae, looking for nectar. These include sulphurs, question marks, painted ladies, skippers, buckeyes, and fritillaries. Daisies aren't as important as larval plants, but painted ladies, pearl crescents, and blues do use them as food for their larvae. Songbirds also visit the plants for seed in winter and hummingbirds visit many species for nectar.

The late summer to fall flowers of wild and cultivated asters, including New England aster *(Aster novae-angliae)* and New York aster *(A. novae-beglii)* feature characteristic daisy flowers with yellow centers and purple, white, or pink ray florets. They provide an important nectar source for adults, along with other late-blooming daisy-family members, including sneezeweed *(Helenium autumnale),* annual and perennial sunflowers *(Helianthus* spp.), and goldenrods *(Solidago* spp.).

Summer-blooming daisies for a butterfly garden include coreopsis or tick-seed *(Coreopsis* spp.), annual and perennial cornflowers *(Centaurea* spp.), oxeye daisies *(Chrysanthemum leucanthemum),* Shasta daisy *(C. maximum),* oxeye *(Heliopsis helianthoides),* fleabanes *(Erigeron* spp.), blanket flowers *(Gaillardia* spp.), senecios or groundsels *(Senecio* spp.), black-eyed Susans *(Rudbeckia* spp.), and purple coneflowers *(Echinacea* spp.).

Yarrow *(Achillea* spp.), Joe-Pye weed *(Eupatorium* spp.), hardy ageratum *(Ageratum houstonianum),* and ironweed *(Vernonia* spp.) also are members of this large family, although their clusters of tiny blooms don't look particularly daisy-like. Gayfeathers *(Liatris* spp.) bear tall stalks of flowers covered with woolly-looking flowers.

In addition to annual sunflowers, several other popular annuals belong to this group and make great additions to a butterfly garden. The following plants are ideal for providing a summer-long supply of flowers: cornflowers or bachelor's button *(Centaurea cyanus),* cosmos *(Cosmos* spp.), Mexican hat *(Ratibida columnifera),* Mexican sunflowers *(Tithonia rotundifolia),* marigolds *(Tagetes* spp.), and zinnias *(Zinnia* spp.).

Several daisy-family members that are considered weeds also attract butterflies. Consider growing them in meadows, along fencerows, or in other appropriate areas. These include beggar-ticks *(Bidens* spp.), hawkweeds *(Hieracium* spp.), dandelions *(Taraxacum officinale),* and thistles *(Cirsium* spp.).

It would be difficult indeed to plan a flower garden — much less a butterfly garden — without including some members of this large tribe. They're beloved additions to beds, borders, and meadows everywhere. Most species thrive in full sun with average to rich soil that is well drained.

Peas, Clovers, and Other Legumes. Members of the pea family, Leguminosae, are good nectar sources for many butterflies, but should also be included in every butterfly garden because they are important plants for butterfly larvae. Sulphurs, blues, and skippers are among the butterflies that use them as food for their larvae. Conventional garden plants that fall into this family include sweet peas *(Lathyrus* spp., including perennial pea, *L. latifolius)* and lupines *(Lupinus* spp.).

Red clover (Trifolium pratense) *is a common meadow inhabitant that attracts painted ladies and a variety of other butterflies.*

Bloodflower (Asclepias curassavica) *is a tender perennial milkweed that can be grown as an annual.*

Alfalfa *(Medicago sativa)* and clovers (sweet clovers, *Melilotus* spp., and *Trifolium* spp.) are both good nectar plants.

Several leguminous trees, shrubs, and vines host butterfly larvae and adults, including false indigo (*Amorpha* spp.), senna or shower tree (*Cassia* spp.), locusts (*Robinia* spp.), indigo-bushes (*Dalea* spp.), indigos (*Indigofera* spp.), mesquite (*Prosopis* spp.), redbuds (*Cercis* spp.), and wisterias (*Wisteria* spp.). Beans, including scarlet runner beans *(Phaseolus coccineus),* which also attract hummingbirds, and broad beans *(Vicia faba)* and other vetches, including *Vicia* spp., crown vetch *(Coronilla varia),* and milk vetch (*Astragalus* spp.), are also in this family.

Most legumes thrive in full sun with average to poor soil. All share the ability to fix atmospheric nitrogen, so they will grow well even in soil that is not very fertile.

Mints. Members of the mint family, Labiatae, feature square stems and spikes of small, two-lipped flowers that attract both butterflies and beneficial insects. The pungent leaves of many mints make them beloved herb garden plants. These include true mints (*Mentha* spp.), hyssops (*Agastache* spp.), lavenders (*Lavandula* spp.), catnip and catmints (*Nepeta* spp.), rosemary *(Rosmarinus officinalis),* and thymes (*Thymus* spp.). Prunella *(Prunella vulgaris)* is a mint-family ground cover. Two mints are also essential hummingbird-garden plants: bee balm (*Monarda* spp.) and sages and salvias (*Salvia* spp.). Both are as at home in the herb garden as they are in the flower garden.

Mints thrive in full sun. Most prefer rich, moist, well-drained soil. Many mints are vigorous plants that can quickly overtake a garden. Grow true mints, hyssops, and bee balms in a spot where their spreading won't pose problems. Or, to control their wandering roots, plant them in bottomless buckets or tubs sunk in the soil.

Milkweeds. Monarch butterflies are perhaps the best-known visitors to members of the milkweed family, Asclepiadaceae, but many other species dine on their nectar as well, including swallowtails, sulphurs, fritillaries, painted ladies, viceroys, skippers, and question marks. Queens also lay eggs on milkweeds. Perhaps the best-known garden flower in the milkweed family is butterfly weed, *Asclepias tuberosa,* which fits as nicely in meadows and wild gardens as it does in borders. Other cultivated milkweeds include bloodflower *(A. curassavica),* an annual, as well as swamp milkweed *(A. incarnata)* and showy milkweed, both perennials.

Most milkweeds require full sun with average, loamy or sandy soil that is well drained. Swamp milkweed will survive in dry soil, but prefers evenly moist conditions.

Painted lady butterfly (shown actual size)

*Black swallowtail butterfly
(shown actual size)*

*Dill is one member of the parsley family that swallowtail larvae feed on. Others are
parsley, Queen-Anne's-lace, and fennel.*

Parsleys. Plants in the parsley or carrot family, Umbelliferae, are especially attractive to swallowtails. Eastern black swallowtails and anise swallowtails, as well as several other species, lay their eggs on parsley *(Petroselinum crispum)*, dill *(Anethum graveolens)*, and Queen-Anne's-lace *(Daucus carota)*. Both Eastern black swallowtails and gray hairstreaks visit the flowers of Queen-Anne's-lace for nectar. Fennel *(Foeniculum vulgare)* and wild parsnip *(Pastinaca sativa)* are two other members of this family.

Grow parsley-family members in full sun in average to rich, well-drained soil. Be sure to plant enough for both you and the butterflies to enjoy. Protect dill and parsley plants you want to keep for your own harvest with floating row covers or netting to keep adults from laying eggs on them. Or gently move larvae you spot on your own plants to butterfly plantings of the same species or to Queen-Anne's-lace or wild parsnip plants growing nearby.

*Gulf fritillary butterfly
(shown actual size)*

Violets and Pansies. Violets and pansies make charming additions to any garden and are especially useful in a garden designed to attract butterflies. Several species of fritillaries lay eggs on these diminutive plants, and spring azures visit the flowers for nectar. Canada violet *(Viola canadensis)*, sweet violet *(V. odorata,* see photo on page 56), and horned violet *(V. cornuta)* are all popular garden perennials.

Violets will grow in sun or shade and prefer a spot with moist soil that is rich in humus. They can become invasive because they self-sow with abandon.

More Flowers for Butterflies

Butterflies visit a wide range of flowers for nectar. Here are some more flowers to consider for your butterfly garden. A bird symbol (🐦) indicates that hummingbirds will also visit the flowers.

Annuals
Antirrhinum spp. Snapdragons. 🐦
Cleome hasslerana. Spider flower. 🐦
Dianthus barbatus. Sweet William. 🐦

Miriabilis jalapa. Four-o'clocks, marvel-of-Peru. 🐦
Nicotiana alata. Flowering tobacco. 🐦
Petunia spp. Petunias. 🐦

Perennials
Alcea rosea. Hollyhocks. 🐦
Allium spp. Onions, garlic.
Astilbe spp. Astilbe.
Camassia spp. Camassia.

Showy sedum *(Sedum spectabile)*

Campanula spp. Bellflowers.

Centranthus ruber. Jupiter's-beard, red valerian.

Dianthus spp. Pinks.

Eriogonum spp. Buckwheats.

Filipendula spp. Queen-of-the-prairie.

Geranium spp. Hardy geraniums.

Heliotropium arborescens. Heliotrope, cherry pie.

Hemerocallis spp. Daylilies.

Hibiscus spp. Hibiscus.

Lantana spp. Lantanas.

Limonium spp. Sea lavenders.

Lobelia spp. Cardinal flower, lobelia.

Penstemon spp. Penstemons.

Phlox spp. Phlox.

Scabiosa spp. Sweet scabious.

Sedum spp. Sedum. Especially *S. spectabile.*

Thalictrum spp. Thalictrum, meadow rue.

Yucca spp. Yucca, Adam's-needle.

Oval-leaved buckwheat (*Eriogonum ovalifolium*)

Mustards and Other Crucifers. The mustard family, Cruciferae, presents something of a battleground between the goals of conventional gardening and butterfly gardening. As its name suggests, the cabbage white butterfly feeds on cabbages and many other members of the mustard family, including broccoli, cauliflower, and kale. Other species of whites and long-tailed skippers visit other mustard-family members, including basket-of-gold *(Aurinia saxatilis)*, sea kale *(Crambe maritima)*, wallflowers *(Cherianthus* spp.), dame's rocket *(Hesperis matronalis)*, and sweet alyssum *(Lobularia maritima)*.

Use floating row covers to keep adult butterflies from laying eggs on cabbages and other crops. Simply spread the row covers loosely over the plants at planting time. "Tuck in" the edges all around with soil to prevent pests from getting access to the plants.

Butterflies visit the flowers of several species of buckeyes. This is bottlebrush buckeye (Aesculus parviflora), *a spreading shrub that reaches about 10 feet in height.*

*Queen butterfly
(shown actual size)*

TREES, SHRUBS, AND VINES FOR BUTTERFLIES

Butterflies visit many different trees, shrubs, and vines, both for nectar and to lay eggs. In fact, some of the most important plants for butterfly larvae are trees. Willows (*Salix* spp.) and aspens and poplars (*Populus* spp.) host the larvae of western tiger swallowtails, mourning cloaks, white admirals, red-spotted purples, and viceroys. Hackberries (*Celtis* spp.) host hackberry butterflies, as well as question marks, and mourning cloaks. Honeysuckles (*Lonicera* spp.), sweet pepperbush *(Clethra alnifolia),* mock oranges (*Philadelphus* spp.), pinxterbloom azalea *(Rhododendron periclymenoides),* and elderberries (*Sambucus* spp.) are especially good sources of nectar.

You may already be growing some of the species listed below; many are also important to songbirds and hummingbirds. A flower symbol (❀) indicates a species that is used for both nectar and as food for larvae.

Aesculus spp. Buckeyes.
Alnus spp. Alders.
Amelanchier spp. Serviceberries.
Aristolochia spp. Pipevines. Including *A. durior* (Dutchman's pipe)
    and *A. serpentaria* (Virginia snakeroot).
Asimina spp. Pawpaws.

Betula spp. Birches.

Buddleia spp. Butterfly bush.

Carpinus caroliniana. American hornbeam.

Caryopteris spp. Bluebeard.

Ceanothus spp. Wild lilacs. Including New Jersey tea
     (C. americanus), Rocky Mountain wild lilac
     (C. fendleri), blueblossom *(C. thyrsiflorus)*, snowbush
     (C. cordulatus), and deerbush *(C. integerrimus)*. ✿

Celtis spp. Hackberries. ✿

Citrus spp. Citrus.

Cornus spp. Dogwoods. ✿

Crataegus spp. Hawthorns.

Fraxinus spp. Ashes.

Hibiscus syriacus. Rose of Sharon.

Holodiscus spp. Rock spiraea.

Humulus lupulus. Hops.

Ligustrum spp. Privets.

Lindera benzoin. Spicebush.

Liriodendron tulipifera. Tulip tree.

Magnolia virginiana. Sweet bay.

Malus spp. Apples and crabapples.

Passiflora spp. Passionflowers.

Plantago spp. Plantains.

Platanus. Sycamores.

Populus. Aspens.

Potentilla. Cinquefoils, potentillas. ✿

Prunus spp. Cherries and plums. Including *P. serotina*
     and *P. virginiana.* ✿

Ptelea trifoliata. Hop tree.

Quercus spp. Oaks.

Rhamnus spp. Buckthorns. ✿

Rhus spp. Sumacs. ✿

Ribes spp. Gooseberries. ✿

Robinia spp. Locust trees.

*Buckeye butterfly
(shown actual size)*

Rubus spp. Blackberries and raspberries. ❀

Salix spp. Willows. ❀

Sassafras albidum. Sassafras.

Spiraea spp. Spiraea or bridal wreath.

Syringa spp. Lilacs. ❀

Vaccinium spp. Blueberries. ❀

Viburnum spp. Viburnums.

Vitex agnus-castus. Chaste tree.

Zanthoxylum americanum. Prickly ash.
  Also *Z. clava-herculis,* Hercules' club.

*Clouded sulphur butterfly
(shown actual size)*

*Monarch butterfly
(shown actual size)*

HARDINESS ZONE MAP

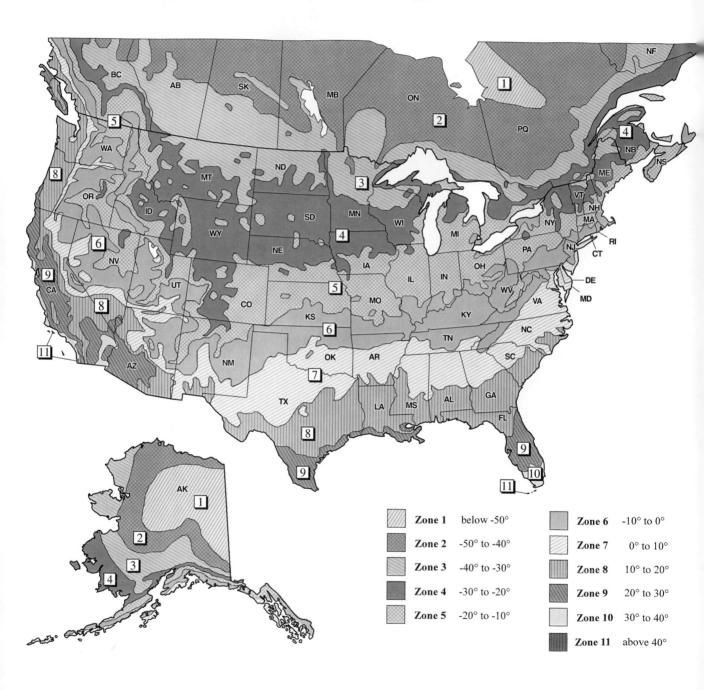

	Zone 1	below -50°		Zone 6	-10° to 0°
	Zone 2	-50° to -40°		Zone 7	0° to 10°
	Zone 3	-40° to -30°		Zone 8	10° to 20°
	Zone 4	-30° to -20°		Zone 9	20° to 30°
	Zone 5	-20° to -10°		Zone 10	30° to 40°
				Zone 11	above 40°

RECOMMENDED READING

Once you have welcomed winged wildlife to your yard, you'll want to get to know your visitors on a first-name basis. Field guides for birds and butterflies, such as books in the Peterson Field Guide Series, are invaluable for identification. A pair of binoculars, kept in a handy place, is useful for getting a better look at both birds *and* butterflies.

Here are some other books that may prove useful in developing a bird and butterfly garden.

Birdscaping Your Garden. George Adams. Emmaus, Pa.: Rodale Press, 1994.

The Butterfly Garden. Jerry Sedenko. New York: Running Heads, 1991.

Building Birdhouses and Feeders. The staff of Ortho Books. San Ramon, Calif.: Ortho Books, 1990.

Butterfly Gardening. The Xerces Society and the Smithsonian Institution. San Francisco, Calif.: Sierra Club Books, 1990.

Gardening for Wildlife. Craig Tufts and Peter Loewer. Emmaus, Pa.: Rodale Press, 1995.

The Hummingbird Book. Donald W. and Lilian Q. Stokes. New York: Little, Brown and Company, 1989.

Landscaping for Wildlife. Carrol L. Henderson. St. Paul, Minn.: Minnesota Department of Natural Resources, 1987.

Woodworking for Wildlife. Carrol L. Henderson. St. Paul, Minn.: Minnesota Department of Natural Resources, 1987.

Recommended Listening

Once you are able to recognize feathered visitors by sight, you may want to learn how to identify them by their songs as well. Cassette tapes of bird songs allow you to listen at your leisure and learn the many songs at your own pace. Two different series are available in the Peterson Field Guide Series. *A Field Guide to Bird Songs* groups songs of related species, with all vireos or owls together, for example. *Birding By Ear* presents groups of songs that sound the same, and a narrator explains similarities and differences to help you learn. Both series are available for eastern and central North America as well as the western region.

Recommended Memberships

You may want to certify your bird and butterfly garden with the National Wildlife Federation's Backyard Wildlife Habitat Program. For an information packet on the program, send $8.45 to National Wildlife Federation, 1400 Sixteenth Street NW, Washington, DC 20036-2266. The packet contains *The Backyard Naturalist,* an 80-page book, along with a pamphlet entitled *Your Backyard Habitat* and other information on the program. (Packets are also available in some wild bird centers.) To certify your yard, you need to fill out a simple form and pay a fee of $15.00.

Photo Credits

Cathy Wilkinson Barash: 65, 86, 106

Gay Bumgarner/PHOTO/NATS: vi–1, 30

Rita Buchanan: 42

Karen Bussolini: 8, 29, 51, 102 right

David Cavagnaro: 7 bottom, 48, 92

Tim Daniel/PHOTO/NATS: 6, 67

R. Todd Davis: 100 right, 108

Barbara W. Ellis: 15, 16, 19, 20, 35, 46, 71, 73

Janet Ellis: 66

Charles Marden Fitch: 55, 90

Stan Green: 11, 21, 54, 79, 80, 97, 104

Dency Kane: 95

Dwight R. Kuhn: iii, 2, 27, 63, 100 left, 102 left

Robert E. Lyons/PHOTO/NATS: 99

Rick Mastelli: 23, 40, 53, 56 bottom, 58, 69, 72, 75, 77, 78, 85, 98, back cover

John Neubauer: 5, 13, 24

Jerry Pavia: 7 top, 56 top

Susan Roth: 9, 60, 83

Laura C. Scheibel/PHOTO/NATS: 89

Joy Spurr: 33, 37, 39, 49, 57, 81, 94

David M. Stone/PHOTO/NATS: 107

INDEX

Titles available in the Taylor's Weekend Gardening Guides series:

Organic Pest and Disease Control	$12.95
Safe and Easy Lawn Care	12.95
Window Boxes	12.95
Attracting Birds and Butterflies	12.95
Water Gardens	12.95
Pruning	12.95

At your bookstore or by calling 1-800-225-3362

Prices subject to change without notice